BALLROOM DANCE

American Style

Smooth - Rhythm - Latin

D1710676

Shirley Rushing
Patrick McMillan

eddie bowers publishing, inc.
2600 Jackson Street
Dubuque, Iowa 52001-3342

ACKNOWLEDGEMENTS

Women's dance wear furnished by:

JNJ Creations
627 Silver Spur Road #210
Rolling Hills Estates, California 90274
(310) 377 6921 telephone
(310) 544-5848 FAX

Students from Trinity University who modeled for photographs:

Reb Bailey
Cara Bowen
Adrienne Cortez
Laurie Grams
Patti Guirao
Brian Huffman
Rich Kannwischer
Gabe Knapp
Sandy Kohn
Katie Lawrence
James Liu
Young-Mee Lee
Matt Mills
Mark Robinson
Jenny Schafer
Jim Smelley
Cindy Wang

eddie bowers publishing, inc.
2600 Jackson Street
Dubuque, Iowa 52001-3342

ISBN 0-945483-58-9

DEDICATION

This book is dedicated to the memory of Edith Gardner, who died on January 25, 1996, after a heroic struggle with cancer. Edith retired from California State University, Sacramento, in 1991 after twenty-two years as a teacher, mentor and visionary in dance and physical education. Her leadership in CAHPERD, AAHPERD, NDA and CBDA resulted in numerous local, state and national awards of recognition.

As the Chair of the College Ballroom Dance Association from 1991 to 1994, Edith was the driving force in the organization and development of the association. Her skill as a leader was unsurpassed. Her ability to define the problem, discard the insignificant and propose a workable solution was an inspiration to all of us.

Edith is remembered by her students for her expertise and for the standards of excellence she inspired in their performance and teaching. Her colleagues remember her for her knowledge of dance and pedagogy, dedication to her profession and willingness to use her talents, skills and energies to serve others.

On a personal note, Edith spent many hours reading, critiquing and making suggestions for this book, for which we shall always be grateful. It is our wish to dedicate this book to the late Edith Gardner and her husband, George, whose continuous support and encouragement contributed to her extraordinary achievement.

INTRODUCTION

This book is the result of a charge to the Standards Comittee of the College Ballroom Dance Association. In August, 1990, at the organizational meeting of the CBDA, the Standards Committee was asked to develop a syllabus for a beginning ballroom dance course. The purpose was an attempt to get agreement from ballroom dance teachers in colleges and universities on content for a beginning class and standardized names for variations.

In 1990-91 a survey was sent to colleges and universities that offered classes in ballroom dance. Teachers were asked to submit their syllabi for a beginning class. It could then be determined which dances and variations were being taught. Names of steps most often used by respondents and leading studios were tabulated and a report was submitted at the CBDA meeting at Brigham Young University in August, 1991. Steps and variations were demonstrated and discussed to determine if members in attendance were in agreement with terminology. In a subsequent meeting using data submitted, members present decided upon core content for beginning classes.

Since colleges have different time commitments for beginning classes ranging from 12-18 weeks and 2 to 3 meetings a week, content will vary. Our objective was to identify and define basic minimum core content for a beginning class. The core curriculum that was agreed upon by CBDA is identified by an asterisk preceding the name of the variation in the contents page. Additional steps for each dance are included following the core.

Suggested musical selections are listed at the end of each dance. Classics that have been popular through the years were chosen over current "pop" songs. Specific bands and labels are not listed as a variety of artists and arrangements are available.

CONTENTS

(RHYTHM DANCES)

(LATIN DANCES)

*Asterisk denotes steps recommended by the College Ballroom Dance Association (CBDA) for beginning class.

BALLROOM DANCE

American Style vs. International Style

American style ballroom dance is the preferred method for teaching beginning dancers in the USA. This book is written in American style. As one progresses through different skill levels (bronze, silver and gold) he/she may be interested in pursuing more instruction in International style. There are similarities and differences in the performance of each style, but usually the objective of American style is social dance and the objective of International style is competition.

Basic differences in the two styles are best differentiated by syllabi (step patterns), dance holds and tempo of the music. American style divisions are smooth and rhythm; International style divisions are standard and Latin. Smooth dances include fox trot, waltz and tango; rhythm dances are swing and polka and Latin dances are rhumba, cha cha, mambo, samba and merengue.

Syllabi for American style dances differ for each studio in the USA. Step patterns are different; terminology is different. However, there are similarities in the performance of the steps. In the bronze syllabi, each step ends with feet together, whereas in silver and gold, the feet are continually passing. In American style men begin the basic step with the left foot; in International style they begin with the right foot.

In International style, Alex Moore's *The Revised Technique* is the syllabi universally accepted. Continuity style (feet passing) is introduced at the beginning level.

In International style partners remain in closed dance position in standard dances. In American style the man may release his partner in order to execute variations. In exhibition dancing and competition partners often separate completely.

Dance tempo is quite specific in international style — fox trot, 30 measures per minute; waltz, 31 measures per minute, and tango, 33 measures per minute. American style allows more variance in speed of the music. Tempi are listed with each individual dance in this text.

There are stylistic differences in step patterns and some similar dances have different names, i.e., jive (International) and swing (American). There are also slight differences in arm and hand holds. At the gold level, or in competition, differences become less significant, sometimes to the point of being unrecognizable.

600 YEARS OF
BALLROOM DANCE

Forerunners of our social ballroom dance were the folk and peasant dances of Europe. These were followed by the court dances taken from peasant-style patterns and dignified by dance masters before being taught to the aristocracy. These dances were concerned primarily with pomp and pageantry. Movements were restricted by heavy, brocaded clothing and grayed in comparison to the free movements, light clothing and simple footwear of the peasants.

The earliest forms of social dance recorded are the medieval basse dances and such Renaissance dances as the pavanne and the galliard. These stately dances were performed between 1400 and 1600, followed by the minuet in the early 1700s. Formal dance at this time belonged totally to the upper classes and was taught and choreographed by dance masters with constrained movements in staged precision.

In the early 1800s, a new, risqué dance was all the rage in Europe: the waltz. A turning dance with a fresh rhythm, the waltz was considered promiscuous and indecent. The man faced his partner, held her in a closed dance position and even placed his hand on her back. Waltzing was a radical move away from the stilted, stand-offish dances of European aristocracy.

In the mid-1800s, a Czechoslovakian dance teacher noted the steps of a wild, spinning dance performed by a peasant girl from Bohemia and introduced it at a village festival; thus, the polka was born. Polka, from the Czech word "pulka," meaning "half-step," refers to the quick change of weight in the "close" step.

The early 1900s introduced the fox trot and the tango. The fox trot, today's most popular dance, originated in 1914 in a New York vaudeville act performed by actor Harry Fox. Fox danced in trotting steps to ragtime music; hence "Fox's Trot." Dance teachers standardized the steps and immediately advertised instruction in the fox trot. The combination of quick and slow rhythms and the abundance of "danceable" music for the fox trot made it America's favorite dance.

The tango, a sensuous dance born in the barrios of Argentina, arrived in America via Spain, France and England. The dance was popularized in America by Rudolph Valentino in the movie "Four Horses of the Apocalypse." Today's tango movements derived from the costumes originally worn by the cortés, full skirts for the women and gaucho suits with boots and spurs for the men.

When African slaves were imported into Cuba several hundred years ago, they brought with them their rhythms, dances and musical instruments. With music influenced by the Spanish and Africans the Cubans have given us several dances which are now categorized as Latin Dances. Originally danced as a ritual pantomime with circular movements imitating the fowl mating ceremony, they have evolved into a pantomime of courtship characterized by a flirtatious attitude and an exaggerated hip movement. Musical instruments that are still a part of our present Latin bands are maracas (gourds containing dry seeds), claves (two sticks struck together) and drums.

The rhumba, cha cha, mambo and merengue have come to us from Cuba and the Caribbean Islands; the samba was imported from Brazil. As American tourism increased in Latin

America and the Caribbean Islands the Latin dances have increased proportionately in popularity. In the big band ballroom dance arena Latin dances now take their place along with the American dances, as most "big bands" play a full complement of Latin music. Some clubs, such as Roseland and the Rainbow Room in New York City, alternate an American band and a Latin band throughout the evening for their dancers.

STYLING

Styling is the unique characteristic of each dance. The styling of each dance is influenced extrinsically by music, costume and tradition. Intrinsic styling is the result of the personality, skill and feeling of the dancer. As skill and confidence develop each dancer will develop an individual style of movement even though all have received the same instruction. Styling for each dance is explained at the beginning of each chapter.

There are styling and performance similarities of dances in the smooth category, and styling and performance similarites of dances in the Latin category. There are also basic differences in the two broad categories. Below are listed some of the differences.

FEET **Smooth:** Feet point straight ahead. Weight is taken on the heel and transferred to the ball of the foot or is taken on the ball or half-toe and transferred back to the entire foot.
Latin: Feet turn out slightly. Weight is taken on the inside ball of the foot and transferred outward to the entire flat foot.

ARMS Man's right arm and woman's left arm are the same in both smooth and Latin, with man's right hand on woman's left shoulder blade and woman's left hand on man's right arm or shoulder.
Smooth: Man's left and woman's right arms are extended with elbows slightly curved. Woman's right hand is held level with her eyes.
Latin: Man's left and woman's right arms are bent at the elbow at approximately 90 degrees. There should be enough space for a fist beteween the elbows.

FOCUS **Smooth:** Focus is over the right shoulder of your partner.
Latin: There is more direct eye contact with your partner, especially in variations that move in a circular pattern.

WEIGHT **Smooth:** Weight is transferred with the step.
Latin: Weight is transferred after the step is taken (Cuban hip motion).

POSTURE

Correct dance posture is a natural outgrowth of proper body alignment. Dancers should assume a tall, relaxed and balanced position. Knees should be slightly flexed, the back should be lengthened and the majority of the weight placed over the balls of the feet. From a side view a plumb line should bisect the ear, shoulder, hip and ankle. The eyes should focus out, looking past the right shoulder of your partner.

LEADING

The basics of leading begin with good body alignment, proper dance frame and the right amount of resistance. Weight is distributed evenly on each foot (75% on toes, 25% on heels) and feet are close together and pointed straight ahead for smooth dances, turned out slightly for Latin dances. Proper dance frame is assumed by the man holding his shoulders down and extending his arms from one elbow to the other. His right hand is placed on the left scapula (shoulder blade) of his partner and his left hand takes her right hand in an extended position. Dance frame is described further in each dance position. The amount of resistance varies with each individual dancer. If the man gives a strong lead his partner must resist with an equal force. A lighter lead allows her to resist less. She should maintain an arm position with a bend in the elbows, always holding the arms firm and never collapsing the shoulder joint. The upper body should initiate the lead moving before the step is taken. If you are counting in a 4/4 pattern, add an "and" between the numbers. Initiate the lead on the "and".

It is the responsibility of the man to initiate and complete a movement pattern. His knowledge of a variety of movement patterns makes dancing more interesting just as one's knowledge of different subject matter makes conversing more interesting.

Although the majority of the lead comes from proper dance frame, the man uses his right hand in assisting the lead in more intricate movements. His left hand constantly assists by exerting pressure. In initiating the lead, the man executes a slight push or pull to move his partner in different directions. Following are listed the directions for reference in the "Lead" column in this book.

R hand heel push
   leads the woman to move directly backward.
L hand hold push
   leads the woman to move directly backward.
R fingers pull
   leads the woman to move directly forward.
L hand hold pull
   leads the woman to move directly forward.
R hand palm push
    leads the woman to move to his left, her right.
R fingertips pull
   leads the woman to move to his right, her left.
R hand hold
   leads the woman to hesitate or to make a transition from one movement into another.
L hand hold
   leads the woman to hesitate or to make a transition from one movement into another.
R hand CW turn
   leads the woman to turn clockwise (right), i.e., promenade and left parallel.
R hand CCW turn
   leads the woman to turn counter-clockwise (left), i.e., right parallel.
L hand hold extends up and out
   prepares the woman for a clockwise "arch" turn.
L hand hold encircles CW
   leads the woman into a clockwise "arch" turn.
L hand hold moves inward and up
   prepares the woman for a counter-clockwise "loop" turn.
L hand hold encircles CCW
   leads the woman into a counter-clockwise "loop" turn.

The man is the "driver" and therefore controls the traffic pattern. He should be able to change the size of his steps and make slight turns in order to blend with the flow of movement. His forward steps should be as long as the music and the height of his partner permit. Sideward steps are smaller and usually do not exceed the shoulder width of his partner. The lead should be firm enough to direct his partner but gentle enough so that it cannot be detected by anyone watching.

It is the man's responsibility to determine which dance is being played, keep time to the music and initiate the lead with his body slightly before taking the first step with his left foot.

FOLLOWING

Just as in leading, the key to being able to follow effectively depends upon good body alignment, the strength of a proper dance frame and the right amount of resistance. The woman should always support her own weight, keep her knees slightly flexed and keep her weight on the balls of the feet. She should know the step patterns and take long steps backward initiating the movement in the hip joint. She should never anticipate, but wait for the initiation of the lead by her partner. Her resistance should be measured by the pressure of his lead. Too much resistance is preferable to not enough. The woman begins with the right foot stepping backward at the beginning of a dance and with the right foot initiating any new movement pattern.

EXERCISES FOR LEADING AND FOLLOWING

The following exercises may be executed by walking in an even rhythm, changing rhythms or executing a basic step.

1. Arm to arm position: man and woman grasp partner's biceps. The man exerts pressure and his partner reacts to his lead.

2. Shoulder position: the woman places her hands on the shoulders of her partner and "receives" the lead. The man's arms are free by his sides.

3. Battle position: the man bends his arms at the elbows, palms up. The woman places her hands on his forearms, palms down.

4. Hand position: both partners bend arms at the elbows and place palms together.

5. Finger position: both partners bend arms at the elbows and place fingertips together.

DANCE POSITIONS
Closed Position

Closed position is used to begin most dances. Partners stand facing each other with the woman standing slightly to the right of the man. Both stand tall with shoulders down and arms comfortably extended from elbow to elbow. He places his right hand on her left scapula (shoulder blade) with fingers together and fingertips pointed diagonally down. His elbow is higher than his wrist and his wrist is higher than his fingertips. His left arm is comfortably extended with hands held at her eye level. His left palm and her right palm face each other with his fingers curling around hers. Her left hand is placed on his right biceps and her left arm is in contact with his right arm. There should be enough space between partners so that each can move freely without feeling that someone is invading his/her space. Focus should be over the right shoulder of each partner. The man establishes the amount of resistance and the woman matches it. Resistance should be constant.

Closed Position (Smooth)

Closed Position (Latin)

Promenade Position

In promenade position the arms remain extended as in closed position. The lead foot (left for man, right for woman) steps to the side with feet turned out approximately 1/8 turn. The second step crosses over. In fox trot and tango bodies face each other; in swing and polka bodies face down the line of dance. Focus is in the direction in which you are moving.

Promenade Position
(Second Step)

7

Parallel Positions

Right parallel position is assumed by each partner moving slightly to his/her side, right shoulders adjacent.

Left parallel position is assumed by each partner moving slightly to his/her side, left shoulders adjacent.

Right Parallel Position

Left Parallel Position

OTHER POSITIONS

Other positions that are used in specific dances are illustrated as the steps are described in the dances.

FOOT POSITIONS

Foot positions are slight variations of foot positions for ballet and modern dance. Pictured here are the five positions depicting Latin (woman's feet) and smooth (man's feet).

1st Position
      Latin: heels are together, toes are turned out slightly.
      Smooth: feet are in parallel position pointing straight forward.

1st Position (Latin)

1st Position (Smooth)

2nd Position

Latin: feet are approximately shoulder width apart with turn-out similar to first position.

Smooth: feet are approximately shoulder width apart pointed straight forward.

2nd Position (Latin)

2nd Position (Smooth)

3rd Position

Latin: heel of one foot is against the instep of the other foot, feet turned out.

Smooth: heel of one foot is against the instep of the other foot, feet turned out from straight forward to 45° angle.

3rd Position (Latin)

3rd Position (Smooth)

4th Position

Latin: feet are separated with heel of one foot in line with toe of the other foot, 45° to 90° turn out.

Smooth: feet are separated with heel of one foot in line with toe of the other foot, feet pointed straight forward at 45° turn out.

4th Position (Latin)

4th Position (Smooth)

5th Position

Latin: feet are together with heel of one foot at right angle to toe of other foot.

Smooth: feet are together, heel of one foot near toe of other foot, feet pointed straight forward at 45° angle.

5th Position (Latin)

5th Position (Smooth)

ETIQUETTE

"May I have this dance?" or "shall we dance?" are proper ways to invite a partner to dance. If the answer is affirmative the man will escort the woman to the dance floor. He will escort her back to her seat after the dance or after a "set" of dances. The woman should never be left on the dance floor alone. Each partner should thank the other at the end of the dance.

If the answer to a request to dance is negative, one should not accept the dance from someone else.

The person leading should "go with the flow" of movement on the dance floor. He should always move in a counter-clockwise direction. If dancing a fast pattern dancers should move to the outside of the floor; those dancing slower patterns should move toward the center of the floor. The man should be able to adjust the size of steps and angle of direction so as to avoid collision with others. In case of accidental collision an apology should be offered immediately. Exhibitions by social dancers are unacceptable. They are designed for entertainment and should be performed at intermission or on stage.

Conversations with other people on the dance floor should be kept to a minimum. A glance of recognition should suffice until the music stops and you can meet off the floor to converse. Your partner should be introduced immediately if you stop to talk with friends. Instruction is for dance classes and should never be given during a dance. Chewing gum on the dance floor is totally unacceptable. This is true for dance classes as well as the most sophisticated ball.

Good body hygiene and oral hygiene are necessary because of the proximity of the dancers. It is not possible to totally disguise a "smoker's breath," but one should take as many precautions as possible such as using mouthwash and breath mints.

Good manners on the dance floor are an extension of good manners in your daily life.

MUSIC

Music for the dances in this book is written in 4/4, 3/4 or 2/4 meter. The denominator (bottom number) indicates the type of note that receives one beat. In each of the three meters above a quarter note receives one beat. The numerator (top number) indicates how many beats there are to a measure.

In each meter an accent is on the first note of the measure. In 4/4 meter a secondary (lesser) accent is on the third beat of the measure. In order to identify the meter one should first listen to the underlying beat (steady pulse). Count the beats in consecutive numbers until you can identify the pattern of accents. The meter should be obvious when you can identify the accent at every fourth (4/4), third (3/4) or second (2/4) note.

In 4/4 music the rhythmical pattern is derived by a combination of slow and quick counts. The slow count gets two beats and the quick count gets one beat. A measure of music in box rhythm for the fox trot is cued "slow (1,2), quick (3), quick (4)". A basic step in magic rhythm for the fox trot is cued "slow (1,2), slow (3,4), quick (1), quick (2)," using 1-1/2 measures of music to complete the step.

The waltz, in 3/4 meter, is cued with the numbers 1, 2, 3. Many people prefer counting one through six to complete a basic step in the waltz. This makes it easier to indicate when movement begins on variations. The most important thing to remember in the waltz is that each step gets the same amount of time. There are no slows and quicks.

The polka is written in 2/4 meter. Without the hop the polka is cued quick, quick, slow, with the quick steps receiving 1/2 beat and the slow step receiving one beat. The polka with the hop is slightly more complicated as the hop will take the last 1/4 of the slow beat. The most popular cue for this step is "1 and 2, ah" ("ah" for the hop) in order to differentiate the timing for the quick steps.

The rhumba, cha cha and mambo are in 4/4 meter. The rhumba has the same timing as the fox trot box rhythm, "slow (1,2), quick (3), quick (4)." The cha cha has three slow counts (1,2,3) and the fourth count is divided (4 &). The mambo holds the first beat of the measure which results in a "quick, quick, slow" rhythm for the three remaining beats.

The samba, in 2/4 meter, uses 3/4 of a beat for the first step, 1/4 for the second step and a full beat for the third step. The merengue, also in 2/4, uses one beat for each step.

In this book the fox trot, tango, swing, rhumba, cha cha and mambo are written in 4/4 meter. The waltz is in 3/4 and the polka, samba and merengue are in 2/4.

At the beginning of each dance, the rhythmical analysis is explained using counts, slow and quick cues and linear notation (horizontal lines indicating the relative time value of each step).

The tempo, or speed of the music, is expressed in the number of measures per minute (MPM) and beats per minute (BPM).

TERMINOLOGY

Against line of dance: moving clockwise around the dance floor.

Alignment: parts of the body in relation to each other.

Arch turn: woman's outside turn to right (clockwise).

Ball change: transfer of weight from the ball of one foot to the flat of the other foot.

Basic step: the step that establishes the rhythm pattern for the dance.

Beat: pulse; a unit of time

Brush: lightly touching the supporting foot with the free foot.

Chassé: a sideways step.

Close: to bring the feet together.

Closed dance position: partners facing each other separated by a small space. Shoulders are parallel, woman slightly to the right of the man, man's right hand placed on woman's shoulder blade, her left hand placed on his right biceps. Man's left hand holds her right hand in an extended position.

Contrary body movement: turning the opposite hip and shoulder toward the direction of movement.

Contrary body movement position: placing a foot across the front or back of the body without turning.

Conversation position: same as promenade.

Cuddle position: woman is on man's right, both facing the same direction. With a double hand hold man's right hand holds woman's left hand at waist level. His left hand holds her right hand at waist level.

Down beat: first beat of the measure.

Draw: closing the free foot to the supporting foot without changing weight.

Fan: a pivoting 1/2 turn in the tango.

Hesitation: a step in which the free foot closes to the weighted foot and is held for one or two beats.

Hop: the body springs into the air beginning on one foot and landing on the same foot.

Left outside position: same as left parallel. (see parallel)

Line of dance: (LOD, also known as line of direction) counter-clockwise direction in which dancers move around the dance floor.

Loop turn: woman's inside turn to the left (counter-clockwise).

Measure: a group of musical beats separated by bars and identified by accents.

Meter: numerical fraction designating number of beats to a measure and type of note that gets one beat.

Open Position: partners facing each other using various hand holds. May be double hand holds or single hand holds, left to right or right to right.

Parallel position: man and woman stand beside each other, left shoulders adjacent for left parallel, right shoulders adjacent for right parallel.

Phrasing: fitting dance patterns to the melody of music.

Pivot: a turn (usually 1/2) made on the ball of the fot.

Promenade position: man and woman are side by side. Man's right hip is adjacent to the woman's left hip and upper torsos form a "V" in smooth dances, a straight line in rhythm dances.

Replace: a change of weight without changing directions.

Rhythm: the pattern made by the regular occurrence of accented and unaccented beats.

Right outside partner: same as right parallel. (see parallel)

Rise and fall: a series of up and down movements, used primarily in the waltz.

Rock: a change of weight on the first step with foot replacement on the second step.

Spot dance: a dance that is executed in one area of the floor (swing) as opposed to moving in the line of dance.

Spotting: focusing on one spot, real or imaginary, during turns in order to avoid or lessen dizziness.

Staccato: a style of performing a musical note or dance movement quickly, briskly, not held.

Step: a change of weight from one foot to the other.

Supporting foot: the weight bearing foot.

Sway: an incline of the body to one side.

Sweetheart position: facing the same direction with the woman on the man's right side, his right hand holds her right hand over her right shoulder. His left hand holds her left hand in front at waist level.

Syncopation: in music, a change of the accent so that it does not fall on the normally accented beat. In dance, performing a movement on the unaccented beat or between beats.

Tempo: speed of music.

Triple step: three steps performed to two beats of music.

Turn out: an outward rotation of the leg and foot initiated at the hip joint.

Upbeat: the last beat of the measure.

Varsouvienne position: same as sweetheart.

Weight change: a transfer of weight from one foot to another, i.e., a walking step.

FOX TROT

FOX TROT

HISTORY

When Harry Fox introduced his "trotting" dance in vaudeville in 1914 his audience was intrigued. It was soon stylized and slowed to a tempo that was "danceable" by the general public. Slow steps were combined with quick steps to make the rhythm pattern more interesting. Dance teachers in New York standardized and advertised. Along with the swing, the fox trot is one of the two dances that is truly American. It is by far the most popular dance in America, comprising approximately 80% of the music played by big bands during an evening of dance.

RHYTHMICAL ANALYSIS

The fox trot is danced to 4/4 meter with a primary accent on the first beat and a secondary accent on the third beat of the measure. The magic rhythm, "slow, slow, quick, quick," was named for Arthur Murray's magic step, so called because of the large number of variations that could be danced in this rhythm. The basic step using the magic rhythm is completed in 1 1/2 measures of music. The box rhythm, "slow, quick, quick," uses two complete measures of music to complete a box step. In each rhythm the slow step gets two beats and the quick step gets one beat. The tempo of the music for the fox trot is slow to medium, 25-45 measures per minute, 100-180 beats per minute.

STYLING

The fox trot is a linear dance that progresses down the line of dance using smooth, controlled steps. The distinguishing characteristic of the fox trot is the brush, lightly touching the inside edge of the supporting foot with the free foot before taking the next slow step. The knees are slightly flexed, the shoulders are back and relaxed and the torso is erect. The slow steps are executed with a heel lead while moving forward and the quick steps are taken with a toe lead to the side. Focus is past the right shoulder of your partner.

FOX TROT

(MAGIC TIMING)

* 1. Basic Step

* 2. Promenade Walk

* 3. Left Rock Turn

4. Promenade with Arch Turn

5. Forward & Backward Parallels

6. Parallel Pivot

(BOX TIMING)

* 7. Box Step

* 8. Left Box Turn

MAGIC STEP ANALYSIS

Man	Forward 1,2	Forward 3,4	Side 1	Close 2	Forward 3,4	Forward 1,2	Side 3	Close 4
	- - - -	- - - -	- -	- -	- - - -	- - - -	- -	- -
	Slow	Slow	Quick	Quick	Slow	Slow	Quick	Quick
Woman	Back	Back	Side	Close	Back	Back	Side	Close

BOX STEP ANALYSIS

Man	Forward 1,2	Side 3	Close 4	Back 1,2	Side 3	Close 4	Forward 1,2	Side 3	Close 4
	- - - -	- -	- -	- - - -	- -	- -	- - - -	- -	- -
	Slow	Quick	Quick	Slow	Quick	Quick	Slow	Quick	Quick
Woman	Back	Side	Close	Forward	Side	Close	Back	Side	Close

17

FOX TROT
Basic Step
(Magic Rhythm)
— Man's Footwork —

Step	Description	Timing	Rhythmic Cue	Lead
1	Step L foot directly **forward** (heel lead). Right foot follows brushing left foot on count 2.	1-2	Slow	R hand heel push
2	Step R foot directly **forward** (heel lead) passing left foot. Left foot follows brushing right foot on count 4.	3-4	Slow	R hand heel push
3	Step L foot **to the left** in line with right foot, shoulder width apart.	1	Quick	R hand palm push
4	Close R foot **to left foot**.	2	Quick	R hand hold

Step #1

Step #2

FOX TROT
Basic Step
(Magic Rhythm)
— Woman's Footwork —

Step	Description	Timing	Rhythmic Cue	Position
1	Step R foot directly **backward**. Left foot follows brushing right foot on count 2.	1-2	Slow	Closed
2	Step L foot directly **backward** passing right foot. Right foot follows brushing left foot on count 4.	3-4	Slow	Closed
3	Step R foot **to the right** in line with left foot, shoulder width apart.	1	Quick	Closed
4	Close L foot **to right foot**.	2	Quick	Closed

Step #3

Step #4

FOX TROT
Promenade Walk
— Man's Footwork —

Step	Description	Timing	Rhythmic Cue	Lead
1	Step L foot **to the left** turning toe outward 1/8 turn into promenade position. Right foot follows brushing left foot on count 2.	1-2	Slow	R hand CW turn
2	Step R foot **forward** in contra body movement position crossing left foot. Left foot follows brushing right foot on count 2.	3-4	Slow	R hand push
3	Step L foot **to the left** returning to closed position.	1	Quick	R hand CCW turn
4	Close R foot **to left foot**.	2	Quick	R hand hold

Step #1

Step #2

FOX TROT
Promenade Walk
— Woman's Footwork —

Step	Description	Timing	Rhythmic Cue	Position
1	Step R foot **to the right** turning toe outward 1/8 turn into promenade position. Left foot follows brushing right foot on count 2.	1-2	Slow	Closed into promenade
2	Step L foot **forward** in contra body movement position crossing right foot. Right foot follows brushing left foot on count 4.	3-4	Slow	Promenade
3	Step R foot **to the right** returning to closed position.	1	Quick	Promenade into closed
4	Close L foot **to right foot**.	2	Quick	Closed

Step #3

Step #4

FOX TROT
Left Rock Turn
— Man's Footwork —

Step	Description	Timing	Rhythmic Cue	Lead
1	Step L foot directly **forward**. Right foot follows brushing left foot on count 2. Weight remains on left foot	1-2	Slow	R hand heel push
2	Step R foot **backward**, toe inward, beginning 1/4 turn left. Left foot follows brushing right foot on count 4. Weight remains on right foot.	3-4	Slow	R fingers pull
3	Step L foot **to the left** completing 1/4 turn counter-clockwise.	1	Quick	R hand palm push
4	Close R foot **to left foot**.	2	Quick	R hand hold

Step #1

Step #2

FOX TROT
Left Rock Turn
— Woman's Footwork —

Step	Description	Timing	Rhythmic Cue	Position
1	Step R foot directly **backward**. Left foot follows brushing right foot on count 2. Weight remains on right foot.	1-2	Slow	Closed
2	Step L foot **forward**, toe outward, beginning 1/4 turn left. Right foot follows brushing left foot on count 4. Weight remains on left foot.	3-4	Slow	Closed
3	Step R foot **to the right** completing 1/4 turn counter-clockwise.	1	Quick	Closed
4	Close L foot **to right foot**.	2	Quick	Closed

Step #3

Step #4

FOX TROT
Promenade with Arch Turn
— Man's Footwork —

Precede with a promenade walk.

Step	Description	Timing	Rhythmic Cue	Lead
1	Step L foot **to the left** turning 1/8 turn counter clock wise into promenade position. Right foot follows brushing left foot on count 2. Raise left hand in preparation for the underarm (arch) position.	1-2	Slow	L hand hold extends up and out, R hand CW turn
2	Step R foot **forward** in contra body movement position crossing left foot. Left foot follows brushing right foot on count 4. Left hand hold encircles partner's head to turn her a full turn clockwise.	3-4	Slow	L hand hold encirles CW, R hand push
3	Step L foot **forward**.	1	Quick	L hand hold lowers
4	Close R foot **to left foot** (3rd position-L foot forward).	2	Quick	R hand hold

Note: Execute a promenade walk to return to closed position. A 3/4 turn may be made end in closed position by stepping side-close on steps 3 and 4.

Step #1

Step #2

FOX TROT
Promenade with Arch Turn
— Woman's Footwork —

Precede with a promenade walk.

Step	Description	Timing	Rhythmic Cue	Position
1	Step R foot **to the right** turning 1/8 turn into promenade position. Left foot follows brushing right foot count 2.	1-2	Slow	Closed into promenade
2	Step L foot **forward** (toe inward) in promenade position pivoting into a full turn clockwise.	3-4	Slow	Arch
3	Step R foot **forward**.	1	Quick	Promenade
4	Close L foot **to right foot** (3rd position-R foot forward).	2	Quick	Promenade

Step #3

Step #4

FOX TROT
Forward & Backward Parallels
— Man's Footwork —

Precede with a basic step.

Step	Description	Timing	Rhythmic Cue	Lead
1	Step L foot **forward** (slightly to the left) Right foot follows brushing left foot on count 2.	1,2	Slow	R hand heel push, L hand push
2	Step R foot **forward** in parallel position. Left foot follows brushing right foot on count 4.	3,4	Slow	R hand heel push, L hand push
3	Step L foot **to the left** turning 1/4 turn to face your partner.	1	Quick	R hand CW turn, L hand push
4	Close R foot **to left foot**.	2	Quick	R hand hold
5	Step L foot **backward** (toe inward) continuing to move down the line of dance. Right foot follows brushing left foot on count 4.	3,4	Slow	R hand CW turn, L hand push
6	Step R foot **backward** passing left foot. Left foot follows brushing right foot on count 2.	1,2	Slow	R hand pull, L hand pull
7	Step L foot **to the left** turning 1/4 turn to face your partner.	3	Quick	R hand CCW turn, L hand pull
8	Close R foot **to left foot**.	4	Quick	R hand hold

Note: Steps 1-8 may be repeated or followed by a left rock turn or basic step.

Step #1

Step #2

FOX TROT
Forward & Backward Parallels
— Woman's Footwork —

Precede with a basic step.

Step	Description	Timing	Rhythmic Cue	Position
1	Step R foot **backward**. Left foot follows brushing right foot on count 2.	1,2	Slow	Closed into right parallel
2	Step L foot **backward**. Right foot follows brushing left foot on count 2.	3, 4	Slow	Right parallel
3	Step R foot **to the right** turning 1/4 turn to face your partner.	1	Quick	Right parallel into closed
4	Close L foot **to right foot**.	2	Quick	Closed
5	Step R foot **forward** turning 1/4 turn moving down the line of dance. Left foot follows brushing right foot on count 4.	3,4	Slow	Closed into left parallel
6	Step L foot **forward**. Right foot follows brushing left foot on count 2.	1,2	Slow	Left parallel
7	Step R foot **to the right** turning 1/4 turn to face your partner.	3	Quick	Left parallel into closed
8	Close L foot **to right foot**.	4	Quick	Closed

Step #5

Step #6

FOX TROT
Parallel Pivot
— Man's Footwork —

Precede with a basic step.

Step	Description	Timing	Rhythmic Cue	Lead
1	Step L foot **forward** (slightly to the left). Right foot follows brushing left foot on count 2.	1,2	Slow	R hand heel push
2	Step R foot **forward** (large step, slightly past your partner) in parallel position. Left foot follows brushing right foot on count 4.	3,4	Slow	R hand heel push
3	Step L foot **to the left** turning slightly more than 1/4 turn to face your partner.	1	Quick	R hand CW turn, L hand push
4	Close R foot **to left foot**.	2	Quick	R hand hold
5	Step L foot **to the left** (toe inward) pivoting approximately 1/2 turn clockwise to face line of dance.	3,4	Slow	R fingers pull
6	Step R foot **in place** (toe outward).	1,2	Slow	R hand hold
7	Step L foot **to the left** in line with right foot.	3	Quick	R hand palm push
8	Close R foot **to left foot**.	4	Quick	R hand hold

Step #5

Step #6

FOX TROT
Parallel Pivot
— *Woman's Footwork* —

Precede with a basic step.

Step	Description	Timing	Rhythmic Cue	Position
1	Step R foot **backward**. Left foot follows brushing right foot on count 2.	1,2	Slow	Closed to parallel
2	Step L foot **backward**. Right foot follows brushing left foot on count 4.	3,4	Slow	Parallel
3	Step R foot **to the right** turning 1/4 turn to face your partner.	1	Quick	Closed
4	Close L foot **to right foot**.	2	Quick	Closed
5	Step R foot **forward** between your partner's feet pivoting approximately 1/2 turn clockwise to back line of dance.	3,4	Slow	Closed
6	Step L foot **around** your partner.	1,2	Slow	Closed
7	Step R foot **to the right** in line with left foot.	3	Quick	Closed
8	Close L foot **to right foot**.	4	Quick	Closed

Step #7

Step #8

FOX TROT
Box Step
— *Man's Footwork* —

Step	Description	Timing	Rhythmic Cue	Lead
1	Step L foot **forward.** Right foot brushes left foot on count 2.	1-2	Slow	R hand heel push
2	Step R foot **to the right** in line with left foot.	3	Quick	R fingertips pull
3	Close L foot **to right foot**.	4	Quick	R hand hold
4	Step R foot **backward.** Left foot brushes right foot on count 2.	1,2	Slow	R fingers pull
5	Step L foot **to the left** in line with right foot.	3	Quick	R hand palm push
6	Close R foot **to left foot**.	4	Quick	R hand hold

Step #1

Step #2

FOX TROT
Box Step
— Woman's Footwork —

Step	Description	Timing	Rhythmic Cue	Position
1	Step R foot **backward**. Left foot brushes right foot on count 2.	1,2	Slow	Closed
2	Step L foot **to the left** in line with right foot.	3	Quick	Closed
3	Close R foot **to left foot**.	4	Quick	Closed
4	Step L foot **forward**. Right foot brushes left foot on count 2.	1,2	Slow	Closed
5	Step R foot **to the right** in line with left foot.	3	Quick	Closed
6	Close L foot **to right foot**.	4	Quick	Closed

Step #3

Step #4

FOX TROT
Left Box Turn
— Man's Footwork —

Step	Description	Timing	Rhythmic Cue	Lead
1	Step L foot **forward** turning toe outward beginning 1/4 turn counter-clockwise. Right foot brushes left foot on count 2.	1,2	Slow	R hand palm push
2	Step R foot **to the right** in line with left foot completing 1/4 turn.	3	Quick	R fingertips pull
3	Close L foot **to right foot**.	4	Quick	R hand hold
4	Step R foot **backward** turning toe inward beginning 1/4 turn counter-clockwise. Left foot brushes right foot on count 2.	1,2	Slow	R fingers pull
5	Step L foot **to the left** in line with right foot completing 1/4 turn.	3	Quick	R hand palm push
6	Close R foot **to left foot**.	4	Quick	R hand hold

Step #1

Step #2

FOX TROT
Left Box Turn
— *Woman's Footwork* —

Step	Description	Timing	Rhythmic Cue	Position
1	Step R foot **backward** turning toe inward beginning 1/4 turn counter-clockwise. Left foot brushes right foot on count 2.	1,2	Slow	Closed
2	Step L foot **to the left** in line with right foot completing 1/4 turn.	3	Quick	Closed
3	Close R foot **to left foot**.	4	Quick	Closed
4	Step L foot **forward** turning toe outward beginning 1/4 turn counter-clockwise. Right foot brushes left foot on count 2.	1,2	Slow	Closed
5	Step R foot **to the right** in line with left foot completing 1/4 turn.	3	Quick	Closed
6	Close L foot **to right foot**.	4	Quick	Closed

Step #3

Step #4

MUSIC FOR FOX TROT

Mack the Knife

Josephine

My Blue Heaven

It Had to Be You

Baubles, Bangles and Beads

Dance in the Old Fashioned Way

The Object of My Affection

There Goes that Song Again

That Old Black Magic

Sweet and Lovely

Marie

I'll Take Care of Your Cares

WALTZ

WALTZ

HISTORY

A legacy from Europe, the waltz had its original roots in the Middle Ages. It was flavored by the "volta" from Italy, the "volte" from France, the "landler" from Austria and took its name from the "waltzen" from Germany. The German word "walzer" meant "sliding or gliding". As the waltz entered the ballrooms of Europe around 1760 it was transformed into a graceful turning flow of movement. The footwork was changed from a step-close-step pattern to our present step-side-close pattern in order to make the dance too complicated for the peasants. In spite of this it was usurped by the commoners and crossed the Atlantic with the immigrants to America. It has been enjoyed by dancers from elegant ballrooms though Broadway musicals to western saloons.

RHYTHMICAL ANALYSIS

The waltz is danced to 3/4 meter with an accent on the first beat of the measure. The rhythm is even, ranging from slow to medium to fast tempo. Since each step gets the same amount of time (one beat) there are no "slow" and "quick" cues. Steps are cued using a repeated "1,2,3" count or "1,2,3,4,5,6" since two measures of music are used to complete a basic step. Music is played at 30-40 measures per minute, 90-120 beats per minute.

STYLING

The waltz is a circular dance. It progresses down the line of dance in a turning motion. The most unique feature of the waltz is the rise and fall. With body erect the first step of the measure uses a heel lead in the forward step. It is initiated with a slightly flexed knee and ends by beginning the rise onto the half-toe. The second step is taken on the half-toe and the third step shifts from the half-toe to the flat foot in order to initiate the next step into the fall. Forward and backward steps are taken directly into your partner. Focus is past the right shoulder of your partner.

WALTZ

* 1. Box Step

* 2. Left Box Turn

* 3. Progressive Box Step

* 4. Underarm (Arch) Turn

* 5. Hesitations: Forward, Backward and Sideways

* 6. Simple Twinkle

  7. Triple Twinkle

  8. Spirals

BASIC BOX ANALYSIS

Man	Forward 1	Side 2	Close 3	Back 1	Side 2	Close 3
	- - - -	- - - -	- - - -	- - - -	- - - -	- - - -
Woman	Back	Side	Close	Forward	Side	Close

WALTZ
Basic Box Step
— Man's Footwork —

Step	Description	Timing	Lead
1	Step L foot directly **forward** (heel to toe).	1	R hand heel push
2	Step R foot **diagonally to the right** in line with left foot (toe).	2	R fingertips pull
3	Close L foot **to right foot** (toe to heel).	3	R hand hold
4	Step R foot directly **backward** (toe).	1	R fingers pull
5	Step L foot **diagonally to the left** in line with right foot (toe).	2	R hand palm push
6	Close R foot **to left foot** (toe to heel).	3	R hand hold

Step #1

Step #2

WALTZ
Basic Box Step
— Woman's Footwork —

Step	Description	Timing	Position
1	Step R foot directly **backward** (toe).	1	Closed
2	Step L foot **diagonally to the left** in line with right foot (toe).	2	Closed
3	Close R foot **to left foot** (toe to heel).	3	Closed
4	Step L foot directly **forward** (heel to toe).	1	Closed
5	Step R foot **diagonally to the right** in line with left foot (toe).	2	Closed
6	Close L foot **to right foot** (toe to heel).	3	Closed

Step #3

Step #4

WALTZ
Left Box Turn
— Man's Footwork —

Step	Description	Timing	Lead
1	Step L foot **forward** turning toe outward beginning 1/4 turn left.	1	R hand palm push
2	Step R foot **to the right** completing turn.	2	R fingertips pull
3	Close L foot **to right foot**.	3	R hand hold
4	Step R foot **backward** turning toe inward beginning 1/4 turn left.	1	R fingers pull
5	Step L foot **to the left** completing turn.	2	R hand palm push
6	Close R foot **to left foot**.	3	R hand hold

Step #1

Step #2

WALTZ
Left Box Turn
— Woman's Footwork —

Step	Description	Timing	Position
1	Step R foot **backward** turning toe inward beginning 1/4 turn left.	1	Closed
2	Step L foot **to the left** completing turn.	2	Closed
3	Close R foot **to left foot**.	3	Closed
4	Step L foot **forward** turning toe outward beginning 1/4 turn left.	1	Closed
5	Step R foot **to the right** completing turn.	2	Closed
6	Close L foot **to right foot**.	3	Closed

Step #3

Step #4

WALTZ
Progressive Box Step
— *Man's Footwork* —

Step	Description	Timing	Lead
1	Step L foot **forward**.	1	R hand heel push
2	Step R foot **diagonally to the right** in line with left foot.	2	R fingertips pull
3	Close L foot **to right foot**.	3	R hand hold
4	Step R foot **forward**.	1	R hand heel push
5	Step L foot **diagonally to the left** in line with right foot.	2	R hand palm push
6	Close R foot **to left foot**.	3	R hand hold

Step #1

Step #2

42

WALTZ
Progressive Box Step
— Woman's Footwork —

Step	Description	Timing	Position
1	Step R foot **backward**.	1	Closed
2	Step L foot **diagonally to the left** in line with right foot.	2	Closed
3	Close R foot **to left foot**.	3	Closed
4	Step L foot **backward**.	1	Closed
5	Step R foot **diagonally to the right** in line with left foot.	2	Closed
6	Close L foot **to right foot**.	3	Closed

Step #3

Step #4

WALTZ
Underarm (Arch) Turn
— Man's Footwork —

Step	Description	Timing	Lead
1	Step L foot **forward**.	1	R hand heel push
2	Step R foot **diagonally to the right** in line with left foot.	2	R fingertips pull
3	Close L foot **to right foot**.	3	R hand hold
4	Step R foot **backward**.	1	R fingers pull
5	Step L foot **diagonally to the left** in line with right foot. Begin to lead your partner under your left hand hold to turn her clockwise.	2	L hand hold extends up and out, R hand palm push
6	Step R foot **to the left**, bringing feet together, continuing to lead your partner under your left hand hold.	3	L hand hold lifts and extends outward

(continued on page 46)

Step #3

Step #4

WALTZ
Underarm (Arch) Turn
— Woman's Footwork —

Step	Description	Timing	Position
1	Step R foot **backward**.	1	Closed
2	Step L foot **diagonally to the left** in line with right foot.	2	Closed
3	Close R foot **to left foot**.	3	Closed
4	Step L foot **forward**.	1	Closed
5	Step R foot **to the right** (toe outward) beginning arch turn.	2	Arch
6	Step L foot **forward** to circle clockwise.	3	Arch

(continued on page 47)

Step #5

Step #6

WALTZ
Underarm (Arch) Turn
— Man's Footwork, cont. —

Step	Description	Timing	Lead
7	Step L foot **forward** continuing arch turn.	1	L hand hold encircles CW
8	Step R foot **diagonally to the right** in line with left foot, continuing arch turn.	2	L hand hold encircles CW
9	Close L foot **to right foot**.	3	L hand hold encircles CW and lowers
10	Step R foot **backward** returning to closed dance position.	1	R hand hold
11	Step L foot **diagonally to the left** in line with right foot.	2	R hand palm push
12	Close R foot **to left foot**.	3	R hand hold

Note: The description above executes the arch turn in place. To turn counter-clockwise, combine the arch turn with the man's footwork of a left box turn.

Step #9

Step #10

WALTZ
Underarm (Arch) Turn
— Woman's Footwork, cont. —

Step	Description	Timing	Position
7	Step R foot **forward** continuing to circle clockwise.	1	Arch turn
8	Step L foot **forward** continuing clockwise circle.	2	Arch turn
9	Step R foot **forward** completing clockwise circle.	3	Arch turn
10	Step L foot **forward** returning to closed position.	1	Closed
11	Step R foot **diagonally to the right** in line with left foot.	2	Closed
12	Close L foot **to right foot**.	3	Closed

Step #11

Step #12

WALTZ
Hesitations: Forward, Backward and Sideways
— *Man's Footwork* —

Step	Description	Timing	Lead
1	Step L foot directly **forward** (heel to toe).	1	R hand heel push
2	Step R foot **forward** bringing feet together (toe). Do not change weight.	2	R hand hold
3	Hold R foot **in place** (toe to heel).	3	R hand hold
4	Step R foot directly **backward** (toe).	1	R fingertips pull
5	Step L foot **backward** bringing feet together (toe). Do not change weight.	2	R hand hold
6	Hold L foot **in place** (toe to heel).	3	R hand hold
7	Step L foot directly **to your left** (toe).	1	R hand palm push
8	Step R foot **to the left** bringing feet together (toe). Do not change weight.	2	R hand hold
9	Hold R foot **in place** (toe to heel).	3	R hand hold
10	Step R foot directly **to your right** (toe).	1	R fingertips pull
11	Step L foot **to the right** bringing feet together (toe). Do not change weight.	2	R hand hold
12	Hold L foot **in place** (toe to heel).	3	R hand hold

Step #1

Step #3

WALTZ
Hesitations: Forward, Backward and Sideways
— Woman's Footwork —

Step	Description	Timing	Position
1	Step R foot directly **backward** (toe).	1	Closed
2	Step L foot **backward** bringing feet together (toe). Do not change weight.	2	Closed
3	Hold L foot **in place** (toe to heel).	3	Closed
4	Step L foot directly **forward** (heel).	1	Closed
5	Step R foot **forward** bringing feet together (toe). Do not change weight.	2	Closed
6	Hold R foot **in place** (toe to heel).	3	Closed
7	Step R foot directly **to your right** (toe).	1	Closed
8	Step L foot **to the right** bringing feet together (toe). Do not change weight.	2	Closed
9	Hold L foot **in place** (toe to heel).	3	Closed
10	Step L foot directly **to your left** (toe).	1	Closed
11	Step R foot **to the left** bringing feet together (toe). Do not change weight.	2	Closed
12	Hold R foot **in place** (toe to heel).	3	Closed

Step #7

Step #9

WALTZ
Simple Twinkle
— Man's Footwork —

Step	Description	Timing	Lead
1	Step L foot **forward**.	1	R hand heel push
2	Step R foot **diagonally to the right** (toe inward) turning 1/8 turn left.	2	R hand CW turn
3	Close L foot **to right foot** in promenade (twinkle) position.	3	R hand hold
4	Step R foot **forward** turning toe outward 1/8 turn.	1	R hand push
5	Step L foot **to the left** in line with right foot to face your partner.	2	R hand CCW turn
6	Close R foot **to left foot**.	3	R hand hold

Step #1

Step #2

WALTZ
Simple Twinkle
— *Woman's Footwork* —

Step	Description	Timing	Position
1	Step R foot **backward**.	1	Closed
2	Step L foot **diagonally to the left** (toe inward) turning 1/8 turn right.	2	Closed to promenade
3	Close R foot **to left foot** in promenade (twinkle) position.	3	Promenade
4	Step L foot **forward** turning toe outward 1/8 turn.	1	Promenade
5	Step R foot **to the right** in line with left foot to face your partner.	2	Promenade to closed
6	Close L foot **to right foot**.	3	Closed

Step #3

Step #4

WALTZ
Triple Twinkle
— Man's Footwork —

Step	Description	Timing	Lead
1-3	Execute steps 1-3 of the simple twinkle.		
4	Step R foot **forward** in promenade position beginning to turn partner counter-clockwise.	1	R hand palm push
5	Step L foot **forward** passing right foot (small step) leading your partner into right parallel position.	2	R hand CCW turn
6	Close R foot **to left foot**.	3	R hand hold
7	Step L foot **backward** in parallel position beginning to turn partner clockwise.	1	R fingers pull
8	Step R foot **backward** passing left foot (small step) leading your partner into promenade position.	2	R hand CW turn
9	Close L foot **to right foot**.	3	R hand hold
10-12	Execute steps 4-6 of the simple twinkle.		

Step #4

Step #5

WALTZ
Triple Twinkle
— Woman's Footwork —

Step	Description	Timing	Position
1-3	Execute steps 1-3 of the simple twinkle.		
4	Step L foot **forward** (toe outward) beginning counter-clockwise turn.	1	Promenade
5	Step R foot **forward** passing left foot pivoting 1/2 turn counter-clockwise.	2	Promenade to right parallel
6	Close L foot **to right foot**.	3	Right parallel
7	Step R foot **forward** (toe outward) beginning clockwise turn.	1	Right parallel
8	Step L foot **forward** passing right foot and pivoting 1/2 turn clockwise.	2	Right parallel to promenade
9	Close R foot **to left foot**.	3	Promenade
10-12	Execute steps 4-6 of the simple twinkle.		

Step #6

Step #7

WALTZ
Spirals
— Man's Footwork —

Step	Description	Timing	Lead
1	Step L foot **forward**.	1	R hand heel push
2	Step R foot **diagonally to the right** (toe inward) turning 1/8 turn left.	2	R hand CCW turn
3	Close L foot **to right foot** in parallel (spiral) position, right shoulder adjacent.	3	R hand hold
4	Step R foot **forward** in right parallel position.	1	R hand heel push
5	Step L foot **to the left** (toe inward) turning 1/4 turn right into left parallel position.	2	R hand CW turn
6	Close R foot **to left foot**, left shoulders adjacent.	3	R hand hold

(continued on page 56)

Step #1

Step #2

WALTZ
Spirals
— *Woman's Footwork* —

Step	Description	Timing	Position
1	Step R foot **backward**.	1	Closed
2	Step L foot **diagonally to the left** (toe outward) turning 1/8 turn counter-clockwise.	2	Closed to right parallel
3	Close R foot **to left foot** in parallel (spiral) position, right shoulders adjacent.	3	Right parallel
4	Step L foot **backward** in right parallel position.	1	Right parallel
5	Step R foot **to the right** (toe outward) turning 1/4 turn clockwise into left parallel position.	2	Right parallel into left parallel
6	Close L foot **to right foot**, left shoulders adjacent.	3	Left parallel

(continued on page 57)

Step #3

Step #4

Step	Description	Timing	Lead
7	Step L foot **forward** in left parallel position.	1	R hand heel push
8	Step R foot **to the right** (toe inward) turning 1/4 turn left into right parallel position.	2	R hand CCW turn
9	Close L foot **to right foot**, right shoulders adjacent.	3	R hand hold
10	Step R foot **forward** in right parallel position.	1	R hand heel push
11	Step L foot **to the left** returning to closed dance position.	2	R hand CW turn
12	Close R foot **to left foot**.	3	R hand hold

Note: Steps 1-3 lead your partner into right parallel (spiral) position.
Steps 4-9 execute a spiral and left spiral. To continue spirals repeat steps 4-9.
Steps 10-12 lead your partner out of spirals and into closed position.

Step #7

Step #8

WALTZ
Spirals
— Woman's Footwork, cont. —

Step	Description	Timing	Position
7	Step R foot **backward** in left parallel position.	1	Left parallel
8	Step L foot **to the left** (toe outward) turning 1/4 turn counter-clockwise into right parallel position.	2	Left parallel into right position
9	Close R foot **to left foot**, right shoulders adjacent.	3	Right parallel
10	Step L foot **backward** in right parallel position.	1	Right parallel
11	Step R foot **to the right** returning to closed dance position.	2	Right parallel into closed
12	Close L foot **to right foot**.	3	Closed

Step #11

Step #12

MUSIC FOR WALTZ

Melody of Love

Isle of Golden Dreams

The Naughty Waltz

Always

Tennessee Waltz

Moon River

Could I Have This Dance

Somewhere My Love

Baubles, Bangles and Beads

Hello Young Lovers

TANGO

TANGO

HISTORY

The most dramatic of the ballroom dances, the tango got its start with the Argentine cowboy. Coming to the United States via Spain, France and England, it was popularized by Rudolph Valentino in the 1920s movie "Four Horses of the Apocalypse". Remnants of the influence of the original costumes, boots and spurs for men, ruffled skirts cut high in front for women, can still be seen in the dance. It has recently seen a revival in the USA through stage concerts of the Argentine Tango.

RHYTHMICAL ANALYSIS

The tango was originally written in 2/4 time but the more popular 4/4 meter is presently used. Accents, primary and secondary, are on the first and third beats of the measure. The basic rhythm is "slow, slow, quick, quick, slow," with the last slow ending in a complete stop, or using the two beats to effect the rhythm change. Tempo of the music is 31-35 measures per minute, 124-140 beats per minute.

STYLING

The styling of the tango is quite unique. The upper body is held erect and the knees remain flexed in order to execute long reaching steps. In closed dance position the man and woman are in closer contact than in other ballroom dances. The first three steps use a strong heel lead for the man. The last slow step may be staccato with a hold or a slow drag using two beats. The woman times her fifth step to correspond to the timing of the man's. Weight is not transferred on the drag step so each succeeding basic step begins on the same foot (left for man, right for woman).

The tango is characterized by fans and cortés. The fan is a half-turn executed by the woman beside the man and, in proper attire, flips her skirt causing a "fan" effect. The corté, popularly called a "dip", is a change of direction where the woman steps forward and the man backward with an exaggerated bent knee. This may be followed by a half-turn which puts the woman into a back extended position looking boldly into the eyes of her partner or coyly toward the floor. Focus varies from looking past and totally ignoring your partner on the basic step to looking deep into his eyes on the corté.

TANGO

* 1. Tango Basic

* 2. Parallel Basic

* 3. Promenade Walk, Left Turn

* 4. Promenade Walk, Right Turn

* 5. Simple Corté

* 6. Medio Corté

  7. La Puerta (Simple)

  8. La Puerta (Double)

TANGO BASIC ANALYSIS

Man	Forward 1,2	Forward 3,4	Forward 1	Side 2	Close 3,4
	- - - -	- - - -	- -	- -	- - - -
	Slow	Slow	Quick	Quick	Slow
Woman	Backward	Backward	Backward	Side	Close

TANGO
Tango Basic
— Man's Footwork —

Step	Description	Timing	Rhythmic Cue	Lead
1	Step L foot **forward**.	1-2	Slow	R hand heel push
2	Step R foot **forward** passing left foot.	3-4	Slow	R hand heel push
3	Step L foot **forward** passing right foot.	1	Quick	R hand heel push
4	Step R foot **diagonally to the right** in line with left foot.	2	Quick	R fingertips pull
5	Close L foot **to right foot** (do not take the weight).	3,4	Slow	R hand hold

Note: Steps 3, 4 and 5 are often cued "tan-go-close."

Step #1

Step #2

TANGO
Tango Basic
— *Woman's Footwork* —

Step	Description	Timing	Rhythmic Cue	Position
1	Step R foot **backward**.	1-2	Slow	Closed
2	Step L foot **backward** passing right foot.	3-4	Slow	Closed
3	Step R foot **backward** passing left foot.	1	Quick	Closed
4	Step L foot **diagonally to the left** in line with right foot.	2	Quick	Closed
5	Close R foot **to left foot** (do not take the weight).	3,4	Slow	Closed

Step #4

Step #5

TANGO
Parallel Basic
— Man's Footwork —

Step	Description	Timing	Rhythmic Cue	Lead
1	Step L foot **forward** (slightly to the left).	1-2	Slow	R hand heel push
2	Step R foot **forward** (outside partner) passing left foot.	3-4	Slow	R hand heel push
3	Step L foot **forward** passing right foot returning to closed position.	1	Quick	R hand heel push
4	Step R foot **diagonally to the right** in line with left foot.	2	Quick	R fingertips pull
5	Close L foot **to right foot** (do not take the weight).	3,4	Slow	R hand hold

Step #1

Step #2

TANGO
Parallel Basic
— Woman's Footwork —

Step	Description	Timing	Rhythmic Cue	Position
1	Step R foot **backward**.	1,2	Slow	Parallel
2	Step L foot **backward** passing right foot.	3,4	Slow	Parallel
3	Step R foot **backward** passing left foot.	1	Quick	Closed
4	Step L foot **diagonally to the left** in line with right foot.	2	Quick	Closed
5	Close R foot **to left foot** (do not take the weight).	3,4	Slow	Closed

Step #4

Step #5

TANGO
Promenade Walk, Left Turn
— Man's Footwork —

Step	Description	Timing	Rhythmic Cue	Lead
1	Step L foot **to the left** (toe outward) into promenade position.	1,2	Slow	R hand CW turn
2	Step R foot **forward** passing left foot (contra body movement) returning to closed dance position.	3,4	Slow	R hand push
3	Step L foot **forward** passing right foot.	1	Quick	R hand push into CCW turn
4	Step R foot **diagonally to the right** in line with left foot.	2	Quick	R fingertips pull
5	Close L foot **to right foot** (do not take the weight).	3,4	Slow	R hand hold

Step #1

Step #2

TANGO
Promenade Walk, Left Turn
— Woman's Footwork —

Step	Description	Timing	Rhythmic Cue	Position
1	Step R foot **to the right** (toe outward) into promenade position.	1,2	Slow	Promenade
2	Step L foot **forward** passing right foot pivoting 1/4 turn to closed dance position.	3,4	Slow	Promenade to closed
3	Step R foot **backward**.	1	Quick	Closed
4	Step L foot **diagonally to the left** in line with right foot.	2	Quick	Closed
5	Close R foot **to left foot** (do not take the weight).	3,4	Slow	Closed

Step #3

Step #4

TANGO
Promenade Walk, Right Turn
— Man's Footwork —

Step	Description	Timing	Rhythmic Cue	Lead
1	Step L foot **to the left** (toe outward) leading your partner into promenade position.	1,2	Slow	R hand CW turn
2	Step R foot **forward** (large step) passing left foot pivoting 1/2 turn clockwise.	3,4	Slow	R hand push
3	Step L foot **to the side** pivoting to face line of dance. Lead partner to step around you.	1	Quick	R hand hold
4	Step R foot **forward** between your partner's feet.	2	Quick	R fingertips pull
5	Step L foot **forward** into promenade position (do not take the weight).	3,4	Slow	R hand hold

Step #2

Step #3

TANGO
Promenade Walk, Right Turn
— Woman's Footwork —

Step	Description	Timing	Rhythmic Cue	Lead
1	Step R foot **to the right** (toe outward) into promenade position.	1,2	Slow	Promenade
2	Step L foot **forward** passing right foot.	3,4	Slow	Promenade to closed
3	Step R foot **forward** between your partner's feet pivoting 1/2 turn clockwise.	1	Quick	Closed
4	Step L foot **to the left** around your partner completing clockwise turn to face line of dance.	2	Quick	Closed
5	Step R foot **forward** into promenade position (do not take the weight).	3,4	Slow	Promenade

Step #4

Step #5

TANGO
Simple Corté
— Man's Footwork —

Step	Description	Timing	Rhythmic Cue	Lead
1	Step L foot **back** with toe out and knee flexed. Right leg remains straight with foot flat on the floor.	1,2	Slow	R fingers pull
2	Return weight **to right foot**.	3,4	Slow	R hand heel push
3	Step L foot **forward** passing right foot.	1	Quick	R hand heel push
4	Step R foot **diagonally to the right** in line with left foot.	2	Quick	R fingertips pull
5	Close L foot **to right foot** (do not take the weight).	3,4	Slow	R hand hold

Step #1

Step #2

70

TANGO
Simple Corté
— Woman's Footwork —

Step	Description	Timing	Rhythmic Cue	Position
1	Step R foot **forward** with flexed knee. Keep left foot in place, toe turned outward, with leg straight. Head looks over left shoulder toward the floor.	1,2	Slow	Closed
2	Return weight **to left foot**.	3,4	Slow	Closed
3	Step R foot **backward** passing left foot.	1	Quick	Closed
4	Step L foot **diagonally to the left** in line with right foot.	2	Quick	Closed
5	Close R foot **to left foot** (do not take the weight).	3,4	Slow	Closed

Step #3

Step #4

TANGO
Medio Corté
— Man's Footwork —

Step	Description	Timing	Rhythmic Cue	Lead
1	Step L foot **forward** (rock step).	1	Quick	R hand heel push
2	**Replace** R foot.	2	Quick	R fingers pull
3	Step L foot **back** with toe out and knee flexed. Right leg remains straight with foot flat on the floor.	3,4	Slow	R fingers pull
4	Return weight **to right foot**.	1,2	Slow	R hand heel push
5	Step L foot **forward** (rock step).	3	Quick	R hand heel push
6	**Replace** R foot.	4	Quick	R fingers pull
7	Step L foot **back** with toe out and knee flexed. Right leg remains straight with foot flat on the floor.	1,2	Slow	R fingers pull
8	Return weight **to right foot**.	3,4	Slow	R hand heel push
9	Step L foot **forward** passing right foot.	1	Quick	R hand heel push
10	Step R foot **diagonally to the right** in line with left foot.	2	Quick	R fingertips pull
11	Close L foot **to right foot** (do not take the weight).	3,4	Slow	R hand hold

Note: Hips and shoulders should face partner.

Step #1

Step #2

TANGO
Medio Corté
— Woman's Footwork —

Step	Description	Timing	Rhythmic Cue	Position
1	Step R foot **back** (rock step).	1	Quick	Closed
2	**Replace** L foot.	2	Quick	Closed
3	Step R foot **forward** with flexed knee. Keep left foot in place, toe turned outward, with head looking over left shoulder toward the floor.	3,4	Slow	Closed
4	Return weight **to left foot**.	1,2	Slow	Closed
5	Step R foot **back** (rock step).	3	Quick	Closed
6	**Replace** L foot.	4	Quick	Closed
7	Step R foot **forward** with flexed knee. Keep left foot in place, toe turned outward, with head looking over left shoulder toward the floor.	1,2	Slow	Closed
8	Return weight **to left foot**.	3,4	Slow	Closed
9	Step R foot **backward** passing left foot.	1	Quick	Closed
10	Step L foot **diagonally to the left** in line with right foot.	2	Quick	Closed
11	Close R foot **to left foot** (do not take the weight).	3,4	Slow	Closed

Step #3

Step #4

TANGO
La Puerta (Simple)
— Man's Footwork —

Step	Description	Timing	Rhythmic Cue	Lead
1	Step L foot **backward** crossing right foot in front of left foot. Lead partner from right parallel into promenade position.	1,2	Slow	R fingers pull into R hand CW turn
2	Step R foot **forward** leading your partner into 1/2 turn counter-clockwise returning to closed position.	3,4	Slow	R hand palm push into CCW turn
3	Step L foot **forward** passing right foot.	1	Quick	R hand heel push
4	Step R foot **diagonally to the right**.	2	Quick	R fingertips pull
5	Close L foot **to right foot** (do not take the weight).	3,4	Slow	R hand hold

1 of Step #1

2 of Step #1

TANGO
La Puerta (Simple)
— *Woman's Footwork* —

Step	Description	Timing	Rhythmic Cue	Position
1	Step R foot **forward** in right parallel position to pivot 1/2 turn clockwise. Left foot extends backward and thighs are kept together.	1,2	Slow	Closed to right parallel to promenade
2	Step L foot **forward** in promenade position pivoting 1/2 turn counter-clockwise.	3,4	Slow	Promenade to closed
3	Step R foot **backward**.	1	Quick	Closed
4	Step L foot **diagonally to the left**.	2	Quick	Closed
5	Close R foot **to left foot** (do not take the weight).	3,4	Slow	Closed

3 of Step #2

Step #3

TANGO
La Puerta (Double)
— Man's Footwork —

Step	Description	Timing	Rhythmic Cue	Lead
1	Step L foot **forward** (rock step).	1	Quick	R hand heel push
2	**Replace** R foot beginning to lead your partner into right parallel position.	2	Quick	R fingertips pull
3	Step L foot **backward** crossing right foot in front of left foot. Lead your partner from right parallel into promenade position.	3,4	Slow	R fingertips pull into CW turn
4	Step L foot **forward** leading your partner into 1/2 turn counter-clockwise returning to closed position.	1,2	Slow	R hand palm push into CCW turn
5	Step L foot **forward** (rock step) passing right foot.	3	Quick	R hand heel push
6	**Replace** R foot beginning to lead your partner into right parallel position.	4	Quick	R fingertips pull
7	Step L foot **backward** crossing right foot in front of left foot. Lead your partner from right parallel into promenade postion.	1,2	Slow	R fingertips pull into CW turn
8	Step R foot **forward** leading your partner into 1/2 turn counter-clockwise returning to closed position.	3,4	Slow	R hand palm push into CCW turn
9	Step L foot **forward** passing right foot.	1	Quick	R hand heel push
10	Step R foot **diagonally to the right**.	2	Quick	R fingertips pull
11	Close L foot **to right foot** (do not take the weight).	3,4	Slow	R hand hold

Step #1

Step #2

TANGO
La Puerta (Double)
— *Woman's Footwork* —

Step	Description	Timing	Rhythmic Cue	Position
1	Step R foot **back** (rock step).	1	Quick	Closed
2	**Replace** L foot.	2	Quick	Closed
3	Step R foot **forward** in right parallel position to pivot 1/2 turn clockwise. Left foot extends backward and thighs are kept together.	3,4	Slow	Closed to right parallel to promenade
4	Step L foot **forward** in promenade position pivoting 1/2 turn counter-clockwise.	1,2	Slow	Promenade to closed
5	Step R foot **back** (rock step).	3	Quick	Closed
6	**Replace** L foot.	4	Quick	Closed
7	Step R foot **forward** in right parallel position to pivot 1/2 turn clockwise. Left foot extends backward and thighs are kept together.	1,2	Slow	Closed to right parallel to promenade
8	Step L foot **forward** in promenade position pivoting 1/2 turn counter-clockwise.	3,4	Slow	Promenade to closed
9	Step R foot **backward**.	1	Quick	Closed
10	Step L foot **diagonally to the left**.	2	Quick	Closed
11	Close R foot **to left foot** (do not take the weight).	3,4	Slow	Closed

3 of Step #3

1 of Step #4

MUSIC FOR TANGO

Blue Tango

Jalousie

Hernandos Hideaway

A Media Luz

La Cumparisita

Tango Verano

El Poeta

Tango Albeniz

La Passionara

El Toreador

SWING

SWING

HISTORY

Swing made its debut at the Savoy Ballroom in New York City in 1927. The music of the fox trot, the dance craze of the early 20s, stimulated the dancers to "break away" from the closed dance position into the open position of the swing. A competitiveness developed among the dancers with couples creating their own steps and attempting to surpass the performances of others.

Originally known as the Lindy Hop after Charles Lindberg's "hop" across the Atlantic to Paris, the swing has gone through many name changes. The jitterbug, shag, jive, boogie woogie and rock 'n roll have all been forerunners of the swing. It was influenced by dances from the 1920s such as the charleston, black bottom, big apple and the shimmy. It later influenced the hully gully, twist and disco hustle of the 60s and 70s.

Swing really "arrived" in the mid-30s simultaneously with the rising popularity of Benny Goodman, the "king of swing" of the big band era. It was popularized around the world during the 1940s through USO clubs by young Americans serving abroad in World War II. In the 50s the swing permeated college campuses across our nation and in the 60s it gave way to individual "do your own thing" dancing. The early 70s experienced a brief disco craze, but by mid 70s to 80s people began returning to "partner" dancing.

RHYTHMICAL ANALYSIS

The swing may be danced in single, double or triple rhythm. Triple rhythm is preferred for medium to fast tempo dances and single rhythm is better suited for very fast music. Both are in 4/4 meter. Rhythm pattern for triple time is (quick, quick, slow, quick, quick, slow, slow, slow,) using 1 1/2 measures to complete a basic step. The "quick" steps get 1/2 beat and the slow steps one beat. The two triple steps take one measure; the two slow (rock) steps take 1/2 measure. All three rhythms are analyzed in detail with basic step descriptions on the following page. Most variations are interchangeable with all rhythm patterns. The tempo of the music is 32-48 measures per minute, 128-192 beats per minute.

STYLING

Body position for the swing is more relaxed than for the other ballroom dances. Dance position is semi-open (comparable to promenade) to open and is referred to as "swing position". The hand hold (man's left, woman's right) is held near the waist with the woman's palm down. The man's fingers are beneath her hand with his thumb on top. This handhold enhances the arch and loop turns that are characteristic of the swing. The swing is executed in one "spot" on the floor as opposed to progressing around the room.

EAST COAST SWING

* 1. Basic Step (Single Time)
* 2. Basic Step (Triple Time)
* 3. Basic Step Turning
* 4. Swing Release
* 5. Throw-Out
* 6. Underarm (Arch) Turn
* 7. Underarm (Loop) Turn
* 8. Side Pass
* 9. Sugar Push
10. Cuddle

BASIC STEP ANALYSIS
(Single Time)

Man	Side	Side	Back	Forward
	1,2	3,4	1	2
	- - - -	- - - -	- -	- -
	Slow	Slow	Quick	Quick
Woman	Side	Side	Back	Forward

BASIC STEP ANALYSIS
(Double Time)

Man	Side	Touch	Side	Touch	Back	Forward
	1	2	3	4	1	2
	- -	- -	- -	- -	- -	- -
	Quick	Quick	Quick	Quick	Quick	Quick
Woman	Side	Touch	Side	Back	Back	Forward

BASIC STEP ANALYSIS
(Triple Time)

Man	Side	Close	Side	Side	Close	Side	Back	Forward
	1	&	2	3	&	4	1	2
	- -	- -	- - - -	- -	- -	- - - -	- - - -	- - - -
	Quick	Quick	Slow	Quick	Quick	Slow	Slow	Slow
Woman	Side	Close	Side	Side	Close	Side	Back	Forward

EAST COAST SWING
Basic Step (Single Rhythm)
— Man's Footwork —

Step	Description	Timing	Rhythmic Cue	Lead
1	Step L foot **to the left** (small step).	1-2	Slow	R hand palm push
2	Step R foot **to the right** (small step).	3-4	Slow	R fingertips pull
3	Step L foot **back** (rock step).	1	Quick	R hand CW turn
4	**Replace** R foot.	2	Quick	R hand CCW turn

Note: Steps 3 and 4 comprise the rock step. When dancing in closed position the rock step is executed at an angle. In open position the rock step moves directly away from your partner.

Step #1

Step #2

EAST COAST SWING
Basic Step (Single Rhythm)
— *Woman's Footwork* —

Step	Description	Timing	Rhythmic Cue	Position
1	Step R foot **to the right** (small step).	1-2	Slow	Swing
2	Step L foot **to the left** (small step).	3-4	Slow	Swing
3	Step R foot **back** (rock step).	1	Quick	Swing
4	**Replace** L foot.	2	Quick	Swing

Step #3

Step #4

EAST COAST SWING
Basic Step (Triple Rhythm)
— Man's Footwork —

Step	Description	Timing	Rhythmic Cue	Lead
1	Step L foot **to the left**.	1	Quick	R hand palm push
2	Close R foot **to left foot**.	&	Quick	R hand palm push
3	Step L foot **to the left** completing a triple step to your left.	2	Slow	R hand palm push
4	Step R foot **to the right**.	3	Quick	R fingertips pull
5	Close L foot **to right foot**.	&	Quick	R fingertips pull
6	Step R foot **to the right** (toe inward) completing a triple step to your right.	4	Slow	R fingertips pull
7	Step L foot **diagonally back** (rock step).	1	Slow	R hand CW turn
8	**Replace** R foot.	2	Slow	R hand CCW turn

Note: All variations are written in triple time.

Step #1

Step #2

EAST COAST SWING
Basic Step (Triple Rhythm)
— Woman's Footwork —

Step	Description	Timing	Rhythmic Cue	Position
1	Step R foot **to the right**.	1	Quick	Closed swing
2	Close L foot **to right foot**.	&	Quick	Closed swing
3	Step R foot **to the right** completing a triple step to your right.	2	Slow	Closed swing
4	Step L foot **to the left**.	3	Quick	Closed swing
5	Close R foot **to left foot**.	&	Quick	Closed swing
6	Step L foot **to the left** (toe inward) completing a triple step to your left.	4	Slow	Closed swing
7	Step R foot **diagonally back** (rock step).	1	Slow	Closed swing
8	**Replace** L foot.	2	Slow	Closed swing

Step #4

Step #7

EAST COAST SWING
Swing Release
— Man's Footwork —

Step	Description	Timing	Rhythmic Cue	Lead
1	Step L foot **to the left** (around your partner) beginning to turn approximately 1/4 turn.	1	Quick	R hand palm push
2	Close R foot **to left foot**.	&	Quick	R hand palm push
3	Step L foot **to the left** completing 1/4 turn.	2	Slow	R hand palm push
4	Step R foot **to the right** releasing right hand hold.	3	Quick	R fingertips pull
5	Close L foot **to right foot**.	&	Quick	L hand hold
6	Step R foot to the right.	4	Slow	L hand hold
7	Step L foot **back** (rock step).	1	Slow	L hand hold push
8	**Replace** R foot.	2	Slow	L hand hold pull

Step #1

Step #2

EAST COAST SWING
Swing Release
— Woman's Footwork —

Step	Description	Timing	Rhythmic Cue	Position
1	Step R foot **diagonally to the right** to circle clockwise.	1	Quick	Swing
2	Close L foot **to right foot**.	&	Quick	Swing
3	Step R foot **to the right** completing 1/4 turn right.	2	Slow	Open swing
4	Step L foot **to the left**.	3	Quick	Open swing
5	Close R foot **to left foot**.	&	Quick	Open swing
6	Step L foot **to the left**.	4	Slow	Open swing
7	Step R foot **back** (rock step).	1	Slow	Open swing
8	**Replace** L foot.	2	Slow	Open swing

Step #3

Step #4

EAST COAST SWING
Throw-Out
— Man's Footwork —

Precede with a basic step.

Step	Description	Timing	Rhythmic Cue	Lead
1	Step L foot **forward** (small step) beginning to lead your partner into open swing position. Lower left hand hold leading partner to move forward with right hand.	1	Quick	L hand hold lowers, R hand palm push
2	Close R foot **to left foot**.	&	Quick	R hand palm push
3	Step L foot **forward** leading your partner into open swing position.	2	Slow	L hand hold
4	Step R foot **to the right** moving parallel with your partner.	3	Quick	L hand hold
5	Close L foot **to right foot**.	&	Quick	L hand hold
6	Step R foot **to the right** completing a triple step.	4	Slow	L hand hold
7	Step L foot directly **back** (rock step).	1	Slow	L hand hold push
8	**Replace** R foot.	2	Slow	L hand hold pull

Note: Steps 1-3 comprise the throw-out movement.
Steps 4-6 move parallel with your partner to your right.
Steps 7-8 comprise the rock step.

Step #1

Step #2

EAST COAST SWING
Throw-Out
— Woman's Footwork —

Precede with a basic step.

Step	Description	Timing	Rhythmic Cue	Position
1	Step R foot **forward** into throw-out.	1	Quick	Promenade
2	Step L foot **forward** passing right foot.	&	Quick	Promenade
3	Step R foot **diagonally to the left** pivoting to face your partner.	2	Slow	Promenade to open swing position
4	Step L foot **to the left** moving parallel with your partner.	3	Quick	Open swing
5	Close R foot **to left foot**.	&	Quick	Open swing
6	Step L foot **to the left** completing a triple step.	4	Slow	Open swing
7	Step R foot directly **back** (rock step).	1	Slow	Open swing
8	**Replace** L foot.	2	Slow	Open swing

Step #3

Step #4

EAST COAST SWING
Underarm (Arch) Turn
— Man's Footwork —

Precede with a basic step or basic step turning in closed position.

Step	Description	Timing	Rhythmic Cue	Lead
1	Step L foot directly **forward** (small step) beginning to lead your partner under your left hand hold.	1	Quick	L hand hold extends up and out, R hand palm push
2	Close R foot **to left foot**.	&	Quick	L hand hold extends up and out, R hand palm push
3	Step L foot **forward** leading your partner to turn clockwise.	2	Slow	L hand hold encircles CW
4	Step R foot **to the right** to in open swing position.	3	Quick	L hand hold lowers
5	Close L foot **to right foot**.	&	Quick	L hand hold lowers
6	Step R foot **to the right** completing a triple step.	4	Slow	L hand hold
7	Step L foot directly **back** (rock step).	1	Slow	L hand hold push
8	**Replace** R foot.	2	Slow	L hand hold pull

Note: Steps 1-3 comprise the arch turn.
       Steps 4-6 move parallel with your partner to your right.
       Steps 7-8 comprise the rock step that moves directly away from your partner.

Step #1

Step #2

EAST COAST SWING
Underarm (Arch) Turn
— Woman's Footwork —

Precede with a basic step or basic step turning in closed position.

Step	Description	Timing	Rhythmic Cue	Position
1	Step R foot **forward** to move under your right hand hold.	1	Quick	Closed swing to open swing
2	Close L foot **to right foot**.	&	Quick	Closed swing to open swing
3	Step R foot **diagonally to the right** pivoting clockwise to face your partner.	2	Slow	Open swing
4	Step L foot **to the left** moving parallel with your partner.	3	Quick	Open swing
5	Close R foot **to left foot**.	&	Quick	Open swing
6	Step L foot **to the left** completing a triple step.	4	Slow	Open swing
7	Step R foot directly **back** (rock step).	1	Slow	Open swing
8	**Replace** L foot.	2	Slow	Open swing

Step #3

Step #4

The loop turn may be preceded by the arch turn, side pass, throw-out or swing release.

Step	Description	Timing	Rhythmic Cue	Lead
1	Step L foot **diagonally to the left** beginning to turn clockwise.	1	Quick	L hand hold pulls inward and up
2	Close R foot **to left foot** continuing to turn your partner counter-clockwise.	&	Quick	L hand hold pulls inward and up
3	Step L foot **to the left** completing a triple step.	2	Slow	L hand hold encircles CCW
4	Step R foot **to the right** moving parallel with your partner.	3	Quick	L hand hold lowers
5	Close L foot **to right foot**.	&	Quick	L hand hold
6	Step R foot **to the right** completing a triple step.	4	Slow	L hand hold
7	Step L foot **back** (rock step).	1	Slow	L hand hold push
8	**Replace** R foot forward.	2	Slow	L hand hold pull

Note: Steps 1-3 comprise the loop turn.
Steps 4-6 move parallel with your partner.
Steps 7-8 comprise the rock step.

Step #1

Step #2

EAST COAST SWING
Underarm (Loop) Turn
— Woman's Footwork —

Step	Description	Timing	Rhythmic Cue	Position
1	Step R foot **diagonally to the left** beginning to turn counter-clockwise under your right hand hold.	1	Quick	Open swing
2	Close L foot **to right foot**.	&	Quick	Open swing
3	Step R foot **diagonally to the left** pivoting to turn counter-clockwise to face your partner.	2	Slow	Open swing
4	Step L foot **to the left** moving parallel with your partner.	3	Quick	Open swing
5	Close R foot **to left foot**.	&	Quick	Open swing
6	Step L foot **to the left** completing a triple step.	4	Slow	Open swing
7	Step R foot **back** (rock step).	1	Slow	Open swing
8	**Replace** L foot.	2	Slow	Open swing

Note: In open swing position the rock step is executed directly away from your partner.

Step #3

Step #4

EAST COAST SWING
Side Pass
— Man's Footwork —

The side pass is usually preceded by the loop turn.
Single hand hold (his left, her right)

Step	Description	Timing	Rhythmic Cue	Lead
1	Step L foot **forward** (toe outward) leading your partner to your right side.	1	Quick	L hand hold pulls inward
2	Close R foot **to left foot.**	&	Quick	L hand hold placed on right side
3	Step L foot **forward** pivoting to complete a counter-clockwise turn to face your partner.	2	Slow	L hand hold releases
4	Step R foot **to the right** moving parallel with your partner. Retake the left hand hold at waist level.	3	Quick	Retake L hand hold
5	Close L foot **to right foot.**	&	Quick	L hand hold
6	Step R foot **to the right.**	4	Slow	L hand hold
7	Step L foot directly **back** facing partner (rock step).	1	Slow	L hand hold push
8	**Replace** R foot.	2	Slow	L hand hold pull

Note: Other names for the side pass are 'hand slide' and 'one hand release.'

Step #1

Step #2

EAST COAST SWING
Side Pass
— *Woman's Footwork* —

Step	Description	Timing	Rhythmic Cue	Position
1	Step R foot **forward** to move past your partner's right side.	1	Quick	Open swing, single hand hold
2	Close L foot **to right foot**.	&	Quick	Open swing
3	Step R foot **forward** pivoting to complete a clockwise turn to face your partner.	2	Slow	Open swing
4	Step L foot **to the left** moving parallel with your partner.	3	Quick	Open swing
5	Close R foot **to left foot**.	&	Quick	Open swing
6	Step L foot **to the left**.	4	Slow	Open swing
7	Step R foot directly **back** facing partner (rock step).	1	Slow	Open swing
8	**Replace** L foot.	2	Slow	Open swing

Step #3

Step #4

EAST COAST SWING
Sugar Push
— Man's Footwork —

Double hand hold.

Step	Description	Timing	Rhythmic Cue	Lead
1	Step L foot **forward**, right shoulders adjacent.	1	Quick	R hand hold extends and pulls, L hand hold pulls inward
2	Close R foot **to left foot**.	&	Quick	R hand hold extends and pulls
3	Step L foot **forward** (toe inward) pivoting clockwise to face your partner.	2	Slow	R hand hold pulls
4	Step R foot **to your right** moving parallel with your partner.	3	Quick	Double hand hold
5	Close L foot **to right foot**.	&	Quick	Double hand hold
6	Step R foot **to the right**.	4	Slow	Double hand hold
7	Step L foot directly **back** facing your partner (rock step).	1	Slow	Double hand hold push
8	**Replace** R foot.	2	Slow	Double hand hold pull

Note: Steps 1-3 comprise the sugar push movement.
Steps 4-6 move parallel with your partner.
Steps 7-8 comprise the rock step.

Step #1

Step #2

EAST COAST SWING
Sugar Push
— Woman's Footwork —

Step	Description	Timing	Rhythmic Cue	Position
1	Step R foot **forward**, right shoulders adjacent.	1	Quick	Open swing to parallel
2	Close L foot **to right foot**.	&	Quick	Parallel
3	Step R foot **forward** (toe outward) pivoting clockwise to face your partner.	2	Slow	Parallel to open swing
4	Step L foot **to the left** moving parallel with your partner.	3	Quick	Open swing
5	Close R foot **to left foot**.	&	Quick	Open swing
6	Step L foot **to the left**.	4	Slow	Open swing
7	Step R foot directly **back** facing your partner (rock step).	1	Slow	Open swing
8	**Replace** L foot.	2	Slow	Open swing

Note: In steps 1-3 arms should remain at elbow level.

Step #3

Step #4

EAST COAST SWING
Cuddle
— Man's Footwork —

Precede with a sugar push.

Step	Description	Timing	Rhythmic Cue	Lead
1	Step L foot **forward** (small step) beginning to lead your partner into 1/2 turn counter-clockwise to your right side.	1	Quick	L hand hold pulls inward and up, R hand hold pushes
2	Close R foot **to left foot**.	&	Quick	L hand hold encircles CCW
3	Step R foot **forward** (small step) completing the lead into cuddle position.	2	Slow	L hand hold encircles CCW
4	Step R foot **backward** (small step) in cuddle position.	3	Quick	L hand hold lowers, R hand hold pulls
5	Close L foot **to right foot**.	&	Quick	L hand hold lowers, R hand hold pulls
6	Step R foot **backward**.	4	Slow	L hand hold lowers, R hand hold pulls
7	Step L foot directly **back** (rock step).	1	Slow	L & R hand holds pull
8	**Replace** R foot.	2	Slow	R forearm push

Note: Steps 1-3 take your partner into cuddle position. Steps 4-6 execute a triple step moving backward. A basic step may be executed in cuddle position moving forward (steps 1-3) and backward (steps 4-6).

Step #1

Step #2

EAST COAST SWING
Cuddle
— Woman's Footwork —

Step	Description	Timing	Rhythmic Cue	Position
1	Step R foot **forward**, right shoulders adjacent, beginning 1/2 turn counter-clockwise under your right hand hold.	1	Quick	Open swing with double hand hold
2	Close L foot **to right foot**.	&	Quick	Open swing
3	Step R foot **diagonally forward** (toe inward) pivoting into cuddle position.	2	Slow	Open swing into cuddle
4	Step L foot **backward** (small step) in cuddle position.	3	Quick	Cuddle
5	Close R foot **to left foot**.	&	Quick	Cuddle
6	Step L foot **backward**.	4	Slow	Cuddle
7	Step R foot directly **back** (rock step).	1	Slow	Cuddle
8	**Replace** L foot.	2	Slow	Cuddle

Step #3

Step #4

EAST COAST SWING
Cuddle
— *Man's Footwork, con't.* —

Step	Description	Timing	Rhythmic Cue	Lead
9	Step L foot **forward** (small step) beginning to lead your partner into 1/2 turn clockwise out of cuddle position.	3	Quick	L hand hold raises, R forearm push
10	Close R foot **to left foot**.	&	Quick	L hand hold encircles CW
11	Step L foot **forward** (small step) leading your partner to face you.	4	Slow	L hand hold encircles CW
12	Step R foot **to the right** moving parallel with your partner.	1	Quick	L hand hold begins to lower
13	Close L foot **to right foot**.	&	Quick	Double hand hold
14	Step R foot **to the right**.	2	Slow	Double hand hold
15	Step L foot directly **back** (rock step).	3	Slow	Double hand hold push
16	**Replace** R foot.	4	Slow	Double hand hold pull

Note: Steps 9-11 take your partner out of cuddle.
Steps 12-14 execute a triple step in open swing position.

Step #9

Step #10

EAST COAST SWING
Cuddle
— Woman's Footwork, con't.—

Step	Description	Timing	Rhythmic Cue	Position
9	Step R foot directly **forward** under your right hand hold beginning to move out of cuddle.	3	Quick	Cuddle
10	Close L foot **to right foot**.	&	Quick	Cuddle
11	Step R foot **forward** (toe outward) pivoting clockwise to face your partner.	4	Slow	Cuddle into open swing
12	Step L foot **to the left** moving parallel with your partner.	1	Quick	Open swing
13	Close R foot **to left foot**.	&	Quick	Open swing
14	Step L foot **to the left**.	2	Slow	Open swing
15	Step R foot directly **back** (rock step).	3	Slow	Open swing
16	**Replace** L foot.	4	Slow	Open swing

Note: Another name for the cuddle is sweetheart wrap.

Step #11

Step #12

MUSIC FOR SWING

In the Mood

Take the A Train

Sweet Georgia Brown

Undecided

Bad, Bad Leroy Brown

Pretty Woman

Pennsylvania 6-5000

Chattanooga Choo Choo

String of Pearls

Boogie Woogie Bugle Boy of Company B

POLKA

POLKA

HISTORY

The polka originated as a Bohemian folk dance in the 1830s. A Czechoslovakian musician was inspired as he watched a young peasant girl sing and dance to an improvised melody. He noted the music, and the dance was later performed as a round dance at village festivals. The name polka came from the Czech work "pulka", meaning half, and referring to the half-step found in the step-close-step foot pattern.

The polka gained popularity in the ballroom after its was introduced as part of a ballet sequence in Paris. Immigrants from Europe introduced it in the USA in the late 1800s. Since it used the same intimate closed dance position as the waltz it created immediate attention and was condemned by conservative religious groups. In spite of puritan condemnation the polka prevailed and it is still a very popular folk and social dance.

RHYTHMICAL ANALYSIS

The polka uses 2/4 meter, two beats to a measure with a quarter note receiving one beat. In the version of the polka without the hop the rhythmic pattern is quick, quick, slow. The first two steps get half a beat each and the third step gets a full beat. In the version of the polka including the hop 1/4 the time value is taken from the full beat. Time value of the beats will be 1/2, 1/2, 3/4, 1/4. Linear notation for each version is illustrated with the basic step.

Tempo of the polka is fast, 40-60 measures per minute, 160-240 beats per minute.

STYLING

The polka is a fast, lively dance with a slight bounce caused by shifting from the flat foot to the ball of the foot. There are many variations, as one can see if you attend a Polish, German, Mexican or Czechoslovakian wedding. The most popular variation in ballroom dance is continuous clockwise turns which allows you to move down the line of dance. The hop varies from leaving the floor to a slight lift of the heel. The body sways into the direction of the turn and posture is relaxed.

POLKA

* 1. Basic Step (Without Hop)

* 2. Basic Step (With Hop)

* 3. Promenade

* 4. Flare

* 5. Right Turns

BASIC STEP ANALYSIS
(Without Hop)

Man	Forward 1	Close &	Forward 2	Forward 1	Close &	Forward 2
	--	--	- - - -	--	--	- - - -
	Quick	Quick	Slow	Quick	Quick	Slow
Woman	Backward	Close	Backward	Backward	Close	Backward

BASIC STEP ANALYSIS
(With Hop)

Man	Forward 1	Close &	Forward 2	Hop ah	Forward 1	Close &	Forward 2	Hop ah
	--	--	- - -	-	--	--	- - -	-
	Quick	Quick	Slow		Quick	Quick	Slow	
Woman	Backward	Close	Backward		Backward	Close	Backward	

POLKA
Basic Step (Without Hop)
— Man's Footwork —

Step	Description	Timing	Rhythmic Cue	Lead
1	Step L foot **forward**.	1	Quick	R hand heel push
2	Close R foot **to left foot** (ball of foot).	&	Quick	R hand heel push
3	Step L foot **forward**.	2	Slow	R hand heel push
4	Step R foot **forward** passing right foot.	1	Quick	R hand heel push
5	Close L foot **to right foot** (ball of foot).	&	Quick	R hand heel push
6	Step R foot **forward**.	2	Slow	R hand heel push

Note: All variations are written without hop.

Step #1

Step #2

106

POLKA
Basic Step (Without Hop)
— Woman's Footwork —

Step	Description	Timing	Rhythmic Cue	Position
1	Step R foot **backward**.	1	Quick	Closed
2	Close L foot **to right foot** (ball of foot).	&	Quick	Closed
3	Step R foot **backward**.	2	Slow	Closed
4	Step L foot **backward** passing right foot.	1	Quick	Closed
5	Close R foot **to left foot** (ball of foot).	&	Quick	Closed
6	Step L foot **backward**.	2	Slow	Closed

Step #3

Step #4

POLKA
Basic Step (With Hop)
— *Man's Footwork* —

Step	Description	Timing	Rhythmic Cue	Lead
1	Step L foot **forward**.	1	Quick	R hand heel push
2	Close R foot **to left foot**.	&	Quick	R hand heel push
3	Step L foot **forward**.	2	Slow	R hand heel push
4	**Hop** on L foot as right knee lifts in front.	Ah		R hand heel push
5	Step R foot **forward** passing left foot.	1	Quick	R hand heel push
6	Close L foot **to right foot**.	&	Quick	R hand heel push
7	Step R foot **forward**.	2	Slow	R hand heel push
8	**Hop** on R foot as left knee lifts in front.	Ah		R hand heel push

Step #1

Step #2

POLKA
Basic Step (With Hop)
— Woman's Footwork —

Step	Description	Timing	Rhythmic Cue	Position
1	Step R foot **backward**.	1	Quick	Closed
2	Close L foot **to right foot**.	&	Quick	Closed
3	Step R foot **backward**.	2	Slow	Closed
4	**Hop** on R foot as left foot lifts in back.	Ah		Closed
5	Step L foot **backward**.	1	Quick	Closed
6	Close R foot **to left foot**.	&	Quick	Closed
7	Step L foot **backward**.	2	Slow	Closed
8	**Hop** on L foot as right foot lifts in back.	Ah		Closed

Step #3

Step #4

POLKA
Promenade
— Man's Footwork —

Precede with a basic step.

Step	Description	Timing	Rhythmic Cue	Lead
1	Step L foot **forward** passing right foot leading your partner into promenade position.	1	Quick	R hand CW turn, L hand push
2	Close R foot **to left foot**.	&	Quick	R hand push
3	Step L foot **forward**.	2	Slow	R hand push
4	Step R foot **forward** passing left foot.	1	Quick	R hand push
5	Close L foot **to right foot**.	&	Quick	R hand push
6	Step R foot **forward**.	2	Slow	R hand push

Step #6 of Basic Step

Step #1

POLKA
Promenade
— Woman's Footwork —

Precede with a basic step.

Step	Description	Timing	Rhythmic Cue	Position
1	Step R foot **forward** turning 1/2 turn clockwise into promenade position.	1	Quick	Closed into promenade
2	Close L foot **to right foot**.	&	Quick	Promenade
3	Step R foot **forward**.	2	Slow	Promenade
4	Step L foot **forward** passing right foot.	1	Quick	Promenade
5	Close R foot **to left foot**.	&	Quick	Promenade
6	Step L foot **forward**.	2	Slow	Promenade

Step #2

Step #3

POLKA
Flare
— Man's Footwork —

Precede with promenade. On the last step of the promenade turn 1/4 turn clockwise to face your partner.

Step	Description	Timing	Rhythmic Cue	Lead
1	Step L foot **to the left**.	1	Quick	R hand palm push
2	Close R foot **to left foot**.	&	Quick	R hand palm push
3	Step L foot **to the left** turning 1/4 turn counter-clockwise to face line of dance.	2	Slow	R hand CW turn
4	Step R foot **forward** passing left foot.	1	Quick	R hand push
5	Close L foot **to right foot**.	&	Quick	R hand push
6	Step R foot **forward**.	2	Slow	R hand push

Note: To repeat flare prepare to face your partner on step 6. Flare is usually repeated three times.

To execute promenade continue to move forward on step 6.

To return to closed position move your partner directly in front of you on step 6.

Step #6 of Promenade

Step #1

POLKA
Flare
— Woman's Footwork —

Precede with promenade. On the last step of the promenade turn 1/4 turn counter-clockwise to face your partner.

Step	Description	Timing	Rhythmic Cue	Position
1	Step R foot **to the right**.	1	Quick	Closed
2	Close L foot **to right foot**.	&	Quick	Closed
3	Step R foot **to the right** turning 1/4 turn clockwise to face the line of dance.	2	Slow	Closed into promenade
4	Step L foot **forward** passing right foot.	1	Quick	Promenade
5	Close R foot **to left foot**.	&	Quick	Promenade
6	Step L foot **forward**.	2	Slow	Promenade

Step #2

Step #3

POLKA
Right Turns
— Man's Footwork —

Precede with right foot turning out (between partner's feet) on step 6 of basic step.

Step	Description	Timing	Rhythmic Cue	Lead
1	Step L foot **to the left** moving aroung your partner 1/4 turn clockwise.	1	Quick	R hand push
2	Close R foot **to left foot**.	&	Quick	R hand **push**
3	Step L foot **to the left** turning toe inward. Pivot on left foot to turn 1/2 turn clockwise.	2	Slow	R hand **push**
4	Step R foot **to the right** (toe outward).	1	Quick	R hand **pull**
5	Close L foot **to right foot**.	&	Quick	R hand **pull**
6	Step R foot **forward** between partner's feet to face line of dance.	2	Slow	R hand **pull**

Note: Repeat steps 1-6 to continue turns.

Step #6 of Basic Step

Step #1

114

POLKA
Right Turns
— Woman's Footwork —

Precede with left foot turning in on step 6 of basic step.

Step	Description	Timing	Rhythmic Cue	Position
1	Step R foot **to the right** turning 1/4 turn clockwise.	1	Quick	Closed
2	Close L foot **to right foot**.	&	Quick	Closed
3	Step R foot **to the right** between partner's feet turning toe outward. Pivot on right foot to turn 1/2 turn clockwise.	2	Slow	Closed
4	Step L foot **to the left**.	1	Quick	Closed
5	Close R foot **to left foot**.	&	Quick	Closed
6	Step L foot **backward**.	2	Slow	Closed

Step #3

Step #4

MUSIC FOR POLKA

Beer Barrel Polka

Clarinet Polka

Pied Piper

Polish and You're Proud

Paloma Blanca

We Like Polka Music

Tic Tac Polka

Let's Dance

Hoop Dee Doo

The Liechtenstener Polka

RHUMBA

RHUMBA

HISTORY

After several attempts to import the rhumba from Cuba into the United States via individual dancers proved unsuccessful, interest was finally stimulated in the late 1920s when Xavier Cugat formed an orchestra that specialized in Latin American music. He opened at the Coconut Grove in Los Angeles and later moved to the Waldorf-Astoria in New York, popularizing Latin American music and dance on both the west and east coasts. The movie, "Rumba," starring George Raft and Carole Lombard, gave Americans a visual image of the new dance in the mid-1930s. It has continued to increase in popularity and is the most popular of all of the Latin dances in the USA.

RHYTHMICAL ANALYSIS

Although the original Cuban rhythm was 2/4 time, it has been "Americanized" into our present 4/4 rhythm. The rhythm pattern is slow, quick, quick, with the accent on the first beat of the measure. The 'slow' step gets two beats and the quick steps get one beat each. Steps are executed on the beat with hip action occurring between the beats. Tempo of the music is 28-34 measures per minute, 112-136 beats per minute.

STYLING

The rhumba is a spot dance that moves in a circular pattern. The distinguishing characteristic is the Cuban hip motion in which weight is shifted from one foot to the other after the step is taken. ("Cuban motion" is described in detail in the rhumba box step.) Partners face each other, feet are turned out slightly and the weight is taken on the inside of the foot and rolled to the outside. The extended arms (man's left, woman's right) are bent at the elbow to approximate a right angle. The "personality" of the rhumba is a dominant male and a defensive but flirtatious female.

RHUMBA

* 1. Rhumba Box

* 2. Left Box Turn

* 3. Crosslead Box

* 4. Fifth Position Break

* 5. Arch Turn

* 6. Cuban Walks (Open)

* 7. Open Break with Arch Turn

8. Forward Rocks

9. Back Spot Turns

BASIC BOX ANALYSIS

Man	Forward 1,2	Side 3	Close 4	Back 1,2	Side 3	Close 4
	- - - -	- -	- -	- - - -	- -	- -
	Slow	Quick	Quick	Slow	Quick	Quick
Woman	Back	Side	Close	Forward	Side	Close

RHUMBA
Rhumba Box (With Cuban Motion)
-Man's Footwork-

Step	Description	Timing	Rhythmic Cue	Lead
1	Place L foot **forward** (partial weight).	1	Slow	R hand heel push
	Shift weight **to left foot**.	2		
2	Place R foot **diagonally to the right** in line with left foot (unweighted).	3	Quick	R fingertips pull
	Shift weight **to right foot**.	&		
3	Close L foot **to right foot** (partial weight).	4	Quick	R hand hold
	Shift weight **to left foot**.	&		
4	Place R foot **backward** (partial weight).	1	Slow	R fingers pull
	Shift weight **to right foot**.	2		
5	Place L foot **diagonally to the left** in line with right foot (unweighted).	3	Quick	R hand palm push
	Shift weight **to left foot**.	&		
6	Close R foot **to left foot** (partial weight).	4	Quick	R hand hold
	Shift weight **to right foot**.	&		

Step #1

Step #2

RHUMBA
Rhumba Box (With Cuban Motion)
-Woman's Footwork-

Step	Description	Timing	Rhythmic Cue,	Position
1	Place R foot **backward** (partial weight). Shift weight **to right foot**.	1 2	Slow	Closed
2	Place L foot **diagonally to the left** in line with right foot (unweighted). Shift weight **to left foot**.	3 &	Quick	Closed
3	Close R foot **to left foot** (partial weight). Shift weight **to right foot**.	4 &	Quick	Closed
4	Place L foot **forward** (partial weight). Shift weight **to left foot**.	1 2	Slow	Closed
5	Place R foot **diagonally to the right** in line with left foot (unweighted). Shift weight **to right foot**.	3 &	Quick	Closed
6	Close L foot **to right foot** (partial weight). Shift weight **to left foot**.	4 &	Quick	Closed

Step #3

Step #4

121

RHUMBA
Rhumba Box Left Turn
-Man's Footwork-

Step	Description	Timing	Rhythmic Cue	Lead
1	Step L foot **forward**, toe out, beginning 1/4 turn left.	1,2	Slow	R hand palm push
2	Step R foot **diagonally to the right** in line with left foot, completing 1/4 turn.	3	Quick	R fingertips pull
3	Close L foot **to right foot**.	4	Quick	R hand hold
4	Step R foot **backward**, toe in, beginning 1/4 turn left.	1,2	Slow	R fingers pull
5	Step L foot **diagonally to the left** in line with right foot, completing 1/4 turn left.	3	Quick	R hand palm push
6	Close R foot **to left foot**.	4	Quick	R hand hold

Step #1

Step #2

RHUMBA
Rhumba Box Left Turn
-Woman's Footwork-

Step	Description	Timing	Rhythmic Cue	Position
1	Step R foot **backward**, toe in, beginning 1/4 turn left.	1,2	Slow	Closed
2	Step L foot **diagonally to the left** in line with right foot, completing 1/4 turn.	3	Quick	Closed
3	Close R foot **to left foot**.	4	Quick	Closed
4	Step L foot **forward**, toe out, beginning 1/4 turn left.	1,2	Slow	Closed
5	Step R foot **diagonally to the right** in line with left foot, completing 1/4 turn left.	3	Quick	Closed
6	Close L foot **to right foot**.	4	Quick	Closed

Step #3

Step #4

RHUMBA
Crosslead Box
-Man's Footwork-

Step	Description	Timing	Rhythmic Cue	Lead
1-3	Execute steps 1-3 of rhumba box turn.			
4	Step R foot **backward**, toe in, beginning 1/4 turn left.	1,2	Slow	R fingers pressure, L hand lowers
5	Step L foot **diagonally to left left** in line with right foot, completing 1/4 turn left.	3	Quick	R fingers pressure, L hand lowers
6	Close R foot **to left foot**.	4	Quick	R fingers pressure, L hand lowers
7	Step L foot **forward**, toe out, beginning 1/4 turn left.	1,2	Slow	R palm push, L hand raise
8	Step R foot **diagonally to the right** in line with left foot completing 1/4 turn left.	3	Quick	R fingertips pull, L hand raise
9	Close L foot **to right foot**.	4	Quick	R hand hold
10-12	Execute steps 4-6 of rhumba box turn.			

Step #4

Step #5

RHUMBA
Crosslead Box
-Woman's Footwork-

Step	Description	Timing	Rhythmic Cue	Position
1-3	Execute steps 1-3 of rhumba box.			
4	Step L foot **forward** moving in front of your partner as he makes 1/4 turn left.	1,2	Slow	Left side to partner
5	Step R foot **forward** continuing movement in front of partner.	3	Quick	Left side to partner
6	Step L foot **forward**; then pivot 1/4 turn left to face your partner.	4	Quick	Left side to partner to closed position
7	Step R foot **backward**, toe in, beginning 1/4 turn left.	1,2	Slow	Closed
8	Step L foot **diagonally to the left** in line with right foot completing 1/4 turn left.	3	Quick	Closed
9	Close R foot **to left foot**.	4	Quick	Closed
10-12	Execute steps 4-6 of rhumba box.			

Step #6

Step #7

RHUMBA
Fifth Position Breaks
-Man's Footwork-

Step	Description	Timing	Rhythmic Cue	Lead
1-3	Execute steps 1-3 of rhumba box.			
4	Step R foot **to the right**.	1,2	Slow	R fingertips pull
5	Step L foot **at right angle** to right foot (left toe to right heel).	3	Quick	R hand CW turn
6	Step R foot **in place**.	4	Quick	R hand CCW turn
7	Step L foot **to the left**.	1,2	Slow	R hand hold releases, L hand hold moves inward
8	Step R foot **at right angle** to left foot (right toe to left heel).	3	Quick	L hand hold extends forward
9	Step L foot **in place**.	4	Quick	L hand hold pulls
10-12	Repeat steps 4-6 above.			
13	Step L foot **forward** making 1/4 turn left.	1,2	Slow	R hand palm push
14	Step R foot **diagonally to the right**.	3	Quick	R fingertips pull
15	Close L foot **to right foot**.	4	Quick	R hand hold
16-18	Execute steps 4-6 of rhumba box.			

Step #4

Step #5

RHUMBA
Fifth Position Breaks
-Woman's Footwork-

Step	Description	Timing	Rhythmic Cue	Position
1-3	Execute steps 1-3 of rhumba box.			
4	Step L foot **to the left**.	1,2	Slow	Closed
5	Step R foot **at right angle** to left foot (right toe to left heel).	3	Quick	Promenade
6	Step L foot **in place**.	4	Quick	Promenade
7	Step R foot **to the right**.	1,2	Slow	Closed
8	Step L foot **at right angle** to right foot (left toe to right heel).	3	Quick	Reverse Promenade
9	Step R foot **in place**.	4	Quick	Reverse Promenade
10-12	Repeat steps 4-6 above.			
13	Step L foot **backward** making 1/4 turn left.	1,2	Slow	Closed
14	Step R foot **diagonally to the right**.	3	Quick	Closed
15	Close R foot **to left foot**.	4	Quick	Closed
16-18	Execute steps 4-6 of rhumba box.			

Step #7

Step #8

RHUMBA
Underarm (Arch) Turn
-Man's Footwork-

Step	Description	Timing	Rhythmic Cue	Lead
1-3	Execute steps 1-3 of rhumba box.			
4	Step R foot **backward**.	1,2	Slow	R fingers pull
5	Step L foot **diagonally to the left**.	3	Quick	L hand hold extends up and out, R hand palm push
6	Close R foot **to left foot**.	4	Quick	L hand hold encircles CW
7	Step L foot **forward** turning toe outward beginning 1/4 turn counter-clockwise.	1,2	Slow	L hand hold encircles CW
8	Step R foot **to the right** in line with left foot completing 1/4 turn.	3	Quick	L hand hold encircles CW
9	Close L foot **to right foot**.	4	Quick	L hand hold encircles CW and lowers
10-12	Execute steps 4-6 of rhumba box, left turn.			

Note: Continue executing rhumba box, left turn.

Step #4

Step #5

RHUMBA
Underarm (Arch) Turn
-Woman's Footwork-

Step	Description	Timing	Rhythmic Cue	Position
1-3	Execute steps 1-3 of rhumba box.			
4	Step L foot **forward** directly into parter.	1,2	Slow	Closed
5	Step R foot **diagonally to the right** beginning to circle clockwise (right).	3	Quick	Arch
6	Step L foot **diagonally to the right** continuing circular pattern.	4	Quick	Arch
7	Step R foot **diagonally to the right** continuing to circle clockwise (right).	1,2	Slow	Arch
8	Step L foot **diagonally to the right** continuing the circular pattern.	3	Quick	Arch
9	Step R foot **diagonally to the right** continuing the circular pattern.	4	Quick	Closed
10-12	Execute steps 4-6 of rhumba box, left turn.			

Step #6

Step #7

129

RHUMBA
Open Cuban Walks
-Man's Footwork-

Step	Description	Timing	Rhythmic Cue	Lead
1-6	Execute steps 1-6 of rhumba underarm (arch) turn.			
7	Step L foot **backward** beginning to circle clockwise.	1,2	Slow	L hand hold lowers to elbow level
8	Step R foot **backward** passing left foot continuing clockwise circle.	3	Quick	L hand hold pull
9	Step L foot **backward** passing right foot continuing clockwise circle.	4	Quick	L hand hold pull
10	Step R foot **backward** passing left foot continuing circle.	1,2	Slow	L hand hold pull
11	Step L foot **backward** passing right foot continuing circle.	3	Quick	L hand hold pull
12	Step R foot **backward** passing left foot completing clockwise circle.	4	Quick	L hand hold pull
13	Step L foot **directly backward** passing right foot leading your partner to face you.	1,2	Slow	L hand hold pull
14	Step R foot **backward** passing left foot.	3	Quick	L hand hold pull
15	Step L foot **backward** passing right foot.	4	Quick	L hand hold pull
16	Step R foot **backward** passing left foot leading your partner into closed position.	1,2	Slow	L hand hold raise, R hand hold
17	Step L foot **diagonally to the left** in line with right foot.	3	Quick	R hand palm push
18	Close R foot **to left foot**.	4	Quick	R hand hold

Step #7

Step #8

RHUMBA
Open Cuban Walks
-Woman's Footwork-

Step	Description	Timing	Rhythmic Cue	Position
1-6	Execute steps 1-6 of rhumba underarm (arch) turn.			
7	Step R foot **forward** beginning to circle clockwise.	1,2	Slow	Reverse Promenade
8	Step L foot **forward** passing right foot continuing clockwise circle.	3	Quick	Reverse Promenade
9	Step R foot **forward** passing left foot continuing clockwise circle.	4	Quick	Reverse Promenade
10	Step L foot **forward** passing right foot continuing circle.	1,2	Slow	Reverse Promenade
11	Step R foot **forward** passing left foot continuing circle.	3	Quick	Reverse Promenade
12	Step L foot **forward** passing right foot..	4	Quick	Reverse Promenade
13	Step R foot **forward** pivoting to face your partner (brush left foot to right foot).	1,2	Slow	Open
14	Step L foot **forward** passing right foot.	3	Quick	Open
15	Step R foot **forward** passing left foot.	4	Quick	Open
16	Step L foot **forward** passing right foot.	1,2	Slow	Open to closed
17	Step R foot **to the right**.	3	Quick	Closed
18	Close L foot **diagonally to right foot**.	4	Quick	Closed

Step #12

Step #13

RHUMBA
Open Break with Underarm (Arch) Turn
-Man's Footwork-

Step	Description	Timing	Rhythmic Cue	Lead
1-3	Execute steps 1-3 of rhumba box.			
4	Step R foot **to the right**.	1,2	Slow	R fingertips pull
5	Step L foot **directly back** (rock step) as left arm extends forward at elbow level (2nd position).	3	Quick	R hand hold releases; L hand hold push and lowers
6	**Replace** R foot.	4	Quick	L hand hold pull
7	Step L foot **to the left** leading your partner into an arch turn.	1,2	Slow	L hand hold extends up and out
8	Step R foot **in 5th position** (right toe at right angle to left heel).	3	Quick	L hand hold encircles CW
9	**Replace** L foot.	4	Quick	L hand hold lowers
10-18	Execute steps 10-18 of fifth position breaks.			

Step #5

Step #7

RHUMBA
Open Break with Underarm (Arch) Turn
-Woman's Footwork-

Step	Description	Timing	Rhythmic Cue	Position
1-3	Execute steps 1-3 of rhumba box.			
4	Step L foot **to the left**.	1,2	Slow	Closed
5	Step R foot **directly back** (rock step) as right arm extends forward at elbow level (2nd position).	3	Quick	Open
6	**Replace** L foot.	4	Quick	Open
7	Step R foot **to the right** (toe outward).	1,2	Slow	Arch
8	Step L foot **across right foot** pivoting 1/2 turn clockwise.	3	Quick	Arch
9	Step R foot **directly in front** of partner.	4	Quick	Arch
10-18	Execute steps 10-18 of fifth position breaks.			

Step #8

Step #10

RHUMBA
Forward Rocks
-Man's Footwork-

Step	Description	Timing	Rhythmic Cue	Lead
1	Step L foot **forward**.	1,2	Slow	R hand heel push
2	Step R foot **forward** (rock step).	3	Quick	R hand heel push
3	**Replace** L foot (rock step).	4	Quick	R fingers pull
4	Step R foot **forward**.	1,2	Slow	R hand heel push
5	Step L foot **forward** (rock step).	3	Quick	R hand heel push
6	**Replace** R foot (rock step).	4	Quick	R fingers pull

Step #1

Step #2

RHUMBA
Forward Rocks
-Woman's Footwork-

Step	Description	Timing	Rhythmic Cue,	Position
1	Step R foot **backward**.	1,2	Slow	Closed
2	Step L foot **back** (rock step).	3	Quick	Closed
3	**Replace** R foot (rock step).	4	Quick	Closed
4	Step L foot **backward**.	1,2	Slow	Closed
5	Step R foot **back** (rock step).	3	Quick	Closed
6	**Replace** L foot (rock step).	4	Quick	Closed

Step #3

Step #4

RHUMBA
Back Spot Turns
-Man's Footwork-

Step	Description	Timing	Rhythmic Cue	Lead
1-6	Execute steps 1-6 of open break.			
7	Step L foot **to the left** circling clockwise.	1,2	Slow	L hand hold pull, R hand hold
8	Cross R foot **behind left foot**.	3	Quick	R fingers pull
9	Step L foot **to the left** circling clockwise.	4	Quick	R fingers pull
10	Cross R foot **behind left foot**.	1,2	Slow	R fingers pull
11	Step L foot **to the left** circling clockwise.	3	Quick	R fingers pull
12	Cross R foot **behind left foot**.	4	Quick	R fingers pull
13	Step L foot **to the left** circling clockwise.	1,2	Slow	R fingers pull
14	Cross R foot **behind left foot**.	3	Quick	R fingers pull
15	Step L foot **to the left** circling clockwise.	4	Quick	R fingers pull
16	Step R foot **to the right**.	1,2	Slow	R fingertips pull
17	Step L foot **behind right foot** in fifth position.	3	Quick	R hand CW turn
18	**Replace** R foot.	4	Quick	R hand palm push into CCW turn
19-24	Execute steps 13-18 of fifth position breaks.			

Step #7

Step #8

RHUMBA
Back Spot Turns
-Woman's Footwork-

Step	Description	Timing	Rhythmic Cue	Position
1-6	Execute steps 1-6 of open break.			
7	Step R foot **forward** between partner's feet.	1,2	Slow	Closed
8	Step L foot **around** partner.	3	Quick	Closed
9	Step R foot **in place** pivoting clockwise.	4	Quick	Closed
10	Step L foot **around** partner.	1,2	Slow	Closed
11	Step R foot **in place** pivoting clockwise.	3	Quick	Closed
12	Step L foot **around** partner.	4	Quick	Closed
13	Step R foot **in place** pivoting clockwise.	1,2	Slow	Closed
14	Step L foot **around** partner.	3	Quick	Closed
15	Step R foot **in place** pivoting clockwise.	4	Quick	Closed
16	Step L foot **to the left**.	1,2	Slow	Closed
17	Step R foot **behind left foot** in fifth position.	3	Quick	Promenade
18	**Replace** L foot.	4	Quick	Promenade
19-24	Execute steps 13-18 of fifth position breaks.			

Step #16

Step #17

MUSIC FOR RHUMBA

Besame Mucho

Spanish Eyes

Amor

Piel Canela

Amapola

Begin the Beguin

Adios

Green Eyes

Tonight

I Talk to the Trees

Yellow Bird

Siboney

CHA CHA

CHA CHA

HISTORY

The cha cha is a relatively new dance compared with the other ballroom dances. It came to us from Cuba in the early 1950s as a variation of the mambo. Two quick weight changes (4 and) replaced the fourth beat of the measure of the mambo making the rhythm easier to understand for American tourists. The name "cha cha" came from the verbal cue used for the rhythmical link from one measure to the next, originally cued as cha-cha-cha.

RHYTHMICAL ANALYSIS

The cha cha is written in 4/4 time with a rhythmical link between the end of one measure and the beginning of the next. A lead-in step is taken on the first beat of the measure resulting in a syncopated rhythm with an accent on the second beat. Originally cued as "1,2,cha,cha,cha," it was changed in the 1950s by Arthur Murray in order to facilitate a legitimate count to the 4/4 music. The basic tempo of the music is 26-33 measures per minute, 104-132 beats per minute.

STYLING

The cha cha is a spot dance that is executed in closed and open (shine) positions. Cuban hip motion is utilized throughout the dance. Steps are taken on the flat foot rolling the weight from the inside to the outside of the foot. Forward steps are taken with weight held back and back steps are taken with weight held forward. In the 'back break step' weight is taken on the ball of the foot. There are variations that are executed in open position where the woman uses visual cues.

CHA CHA

* 1. Cha Cha Basic, Turning Left

* 2. Crossover Breaks

* 3. Walk Around Turn

* 4. Parallel Breaks

* 5. Open Break with Underarm (Arch) Turn

* 6. Progressive Basic

* 7. Chase (Half Turn)

* 8. Full Turn

CHA CHA ANALYSIS

Man	Side	Back	Forward	Side	Close	Side	Forward	Back	Side	Close
	1	2	3	4	and	1	2	3	4	and
	- - - -	- - - -	- - - -	- -	- -	- - - -	- - - -	- - - -	- -	- -
	Slow	Slow	Slow	Quick	Quick	Slow	Slow	Slow	Quick	Quick
Woman	Side	Forward	Back	Side	Close	Side	Back	Forward	Side	Close

CHA CHA
Cha Cha Basic
-Man's Footwork-

Step	Description	Timing	Rhythmic Cue	Lead
1	Step L foot **to the left**.	1	Slow	L hand palm push
2	Step R foot **back** (rock step).	2	Slow	R fingers pull
3	**Replace** L foot.	3	Slow	R hand heel push
4	Step R foot **to the right**.	4	Quick	R fingertips pull
5	Close L foot **to the right**.	&	Quick	R hand pressure
6	Step R foot **to the right**.	1	Slow	R fingertips pull
7	Step L foot **forward** (rock step).	2	Slow	R hand heel push
8	**Replace** R foot.	3	Slow	R fingers pull
9	Step L foot **to the left**.	4	Quick	R hand palm push
10	Close R foot **to left foot**.	&	Quick	R hand pressure

Note: To execute cha cha basic turning left, step left foot forward (toe outward) initiating 1/4 turn on step 3. Complete 1/4 turn on steps 4 and 5.

Step #1

Step #2

CHA CHA
Cha Cha Basic
-Woman's Footwork-

Step	Description	Timing	Rhythmic Cue	Position
1	Step R foot **to the right**.	1	Slow	Closed
2	Step L foot **forward** (rock step).	2	Slow	Closed
3	**Replace** R foot.	3	Slow	Closed
4	Step L foot **to the left**.	4	Quick	Closed
5	Close R foot **to left foot**.	&	Quick	Closed
6	Step L foot **to the left**.	1	Slow	Closed
7	Step R foot **back** (rock step).	2	Slow	Closed
8	**Replace** L foot.	3	Slow	Closed
9	Step R foot **to the right**.	4	Quick	Closed
10	Close L foot **to right foot**.	&	Quick	Closed

Note: To execute cha cha basic turning left, step right foot back (toe inward) initiating 1/4 turn on step 3. Complete 1/4 turn on steps 4 and 5.

Step #3

Step #4

CHA CHA
Crossover Breaks
-Man's Footwork-

Step	Description	Timing	Rhythmic Cue	Lead
1-5	Execute steps 1-5 of cha cha basic.			
6	Step R foot **to the right** turning toe outward to begin 1/4 turn right.	1	Slow	L hand hold moves inward, R hand hold releases
7	Step L foot **forward** crossing over right foot.	2	Slow	L hand hold extends forward, R hand extends to right
8	**Replace** R foot beginning 1/4 turn left.	3	Slow	L hand hold pull
9	Step L foot **to the left** to face your partner.	4	Quick	L hand hold pull
10	Close R foot **to left**.	&	Quick	Double hand hold
11	Step L foot **to the left** turning toe outward to begin 1/4 turn left.	1	Slow	R hand hold moves inward, L hand hold release
12	Step R foot **forward** crossing over left foot.	2	Slow	R hand hold extends forward, L hand extends to left
13	**Replace** L foot beginning 1/4 turn right.	3	Slow	R hand hold pull
14	Step R foot **to the right** to face your partner.	4	Quick	R hand hold pull
15	Close L foot **to right foot**.	&	Quick	Double hand hold
*	Repeat steps 6-15 to continue crossover breaks.			
16-20	Execute steps 6-10 of cha cha basic.			

Step #6

Step #7

144

CHA CHA
Crossover Breaks
-Woman's Footwork-

Step	Description	Timing	Rhythmic Cue	Position
1-5	Execute steps 1-5 of cha cha basic.			
6	Step L foot **to the left** turning toe outward to begin 1/4 turn left.	1	Slow	Closed into side by side
7	Step R foot **forward** crossing over left foot .	2	Slow	Crossover
8	**Replace** L foot beginning 1/4 turn right.	3	Slow	Crossover
9	Step R foot **to the right** to face your partner.	4	Quick	Into facing partner
10	Close L foot **to right foot**.	&	Quick	Facing partner
11	Step R foot **to the right** turning toe outward to begin 1/4 turn right.	1	Slow	Facing partner into side by side
12	Step L foot **forward** crossing over right foot.	2	Slow	Crossover
13	**Replace** R foot beginning 1/4 turn left.	3	Slow	Crossover
14	Step L foot **to the left** to face your partner.	4	Quick	Into facing partner
15	Close R foot **to left foot**.	&	Quick	Facing partner
*	Repeat steps 6-15 to continue crossover breaks.			
16-20	Execute steps 6-10 of cha cha basic.			

Step #11

Step #12

CHA CHA
Walk Around Turn
-Man's Footwork-

Note: Walk around turn replaces steps 11-15 of crossover breaks. It usually replaces the 4th crossover. As you begin the turn place your right arm behind your back instead of taking a double hand hold. (A right hand lead may be executed after taking a double hand hold.)

Step	Description	Timing	Rhythmic Cue	Lead
11	Step L foot **to the left** turning toe outward to begin full turn counter-clockwise.	1	Slow	Place L palm to partner's right palm
12	Step R foot **forward** crossing over left foot pivoting one half turn left.	2	Slow	L hand palm push
13	**Replace** L foot pivoting one quarter turn to face your partner.	3	Slow	Visual
14	Step R foot **to the right** to face your partner.	4	Quick	Retake closed position
15	Close L foot **to right foot**.	&	Quick	R & L hand holds
16-20	Execute steps 6-10 of cha cha basic.			

Step #11

Step #12

CHA CHA
Walk Around Turn
-Woman's Footwork-

Note: Walk around turn replaces steps 11-15 of crossover breaks. It usually replaces the 4th crossover. As you begin the turn place your left arm behind your back instead of taking a double hand hold.

Step	Description	Timing	Rhythmic Cue	Position
11	Step R foot to the right turning toe outward to begin full turn clockwise.	1	Slow	Crossover
12	Step L foot forward crossing over right foot pivoting 1/2 turn right.	2	Slow	Crossover
13	Replace R foot pivoting 1/4 turn to face your partner.	3	Slow	Open
14	Step L foot to the left to face your partner.	4	Quick	Closed
15	Close R foot to left foot.	&	Quick	Closed
16-20	Execute steps 6-10 of cha cha basic.			

Step #13

Step #14

CHA CHA
Parallel Breaks
-Man's Footwork-

Step	Description	Timing	Rhythmic Cue	Lead
1-5	Execute steps 1-5 of cha cha basic.			
6	Step R foot **to the right** turning 1/8 turn right (toe out).	1	Slow	R hand CW turn, L hand push
7	Step L foot **forward** crossing in front of right foot.	2	Slow	R hand hold, L hand heel push
8	**Replace** R foot.	3	Slow	R hand CCW turn, L hand pull
9	Step L foot **to the left** making 1/8 turn left to face your partner.	4	Quick	R hand palm push
10	Close R foot **to left foot**.	&	Quick	R hand hold
11	Step L foot **to the left** turning1/8 turn left (toe out).	1	Slow	R hand CCW turn, L hand pull
12	Step R foot **forward** crossing in front of left foot.	2	Slow	R hand heel push
13	**Replace** L foot.	3	Slow	R hand CW turn
14	Step R foot **to the right** making 1/8 turn right to face your partner.	4	Quick	R fingertips pull
15	Close L foot **to right foot**.	&	Quick	R hand hold
*	Repeat steps 6-15 to continue parallel breaks.			
16-20	Execute steps 6-10 of cha cha basic.			

Step #6

Step #7

148

CHA CHA
Parallel Breaks
-Woman's Footwork-

Step	Description	Timing	Rhythmic Cue	Position
1-5	Execute steps 1-5 of cha cha basic.			
6	Step L foot **to the left** turning 1/8 turn right (toe in).	1	Slow	Closed to parallel
7	Step R foot **back** crossing behind left foot.	2	Slow	Parallel
8	**Replace** L foot.	3	Slow	Parallel to closed
9	Step R foot **to the right** making 1/8 turn left .	4	Quick	Closed
10	Close L foot **to right foot**.	&	Quick	Closed
11	Step R foot **to the right** turning 1/8 turn left (toe in).	1	Slow	Closed to parallel
12	Step L foot **back** crossing behind right foot.	2	Slow	Parallel
13	**Replace** R foot.	3	Slow	Parallel to closed
14	Step L foot **to the left** making 1/8 turn right.	4	Quick	Closed
15	Close R foot **to left foot**.	&	Quick	Closed
*	Repeat steps 6-15 to continue parallel breaks.			
16-20	Execute steps 6-10 of cha cha basic.			

Step #11

Step #12

CHA CHA
Open Break with Underarm (Arch) Turn
-Man's Footwork-

Step	Description	Timing	Rhythmic Cue	Lead
1-5	Execute steps 1-5 of cha cha basic.			
6	Step R foot **to the right**.	1	Slow	R fingers pull
7	Step L foot **back** (rock step) as right arm extends forward at elbow level.	2	Slow	L hand hold push, R hand hold release
8	**Replace** R foot.	3	Slow	L hand hold pull
9	Step L foot **to the left**.	4	Quick	L hand hold
10	Close R foot **to left foot**.	&	Quick	L hand hold
11	Step L foot **to the left** leading your partner into an arch turn.	1	Slow	L hand hold extends up and out
12	Step R foot **back**.	2	Slow	L hand hold encircles CW
13	**Replace** L foot.	3	Slow	L hand hold lowers
14	Step R foot **to the right**.	4	Quick	L & R hand holds
15	Close L foot **to right foot**.	&	Quick	L & R hand holds
16-20	Execute steps 6-10 of cha cha basic.			

Step #11

Step #12

CHA CHA
Open Break with Underarm (Arch) Turn
-Woman's Footwork-

Step	Description	Timing	Rhythmic Cue	Position
1-5	Execute steps 1-5 of cha cha basic.			
6	Step L foot **to the left**.	1	Slow	Closed
7	Step R foot **back**.	2	Slow	Closed to open, single hand hold
8	**Replace** L foot.	3	Slow	Open, single hand hold
9	Step R foot **to the right**.	4	Quick	Open, single hand hold
10	Close L foot **to right foot**.	&	Quick	Open, single hand hold
11	Step R foot **to the right** turning toe out.	1	Slow	Arch
12	Step L foot **across right foot** pivoting 1/2 turn right.	2	Slow	Arch
13	**Replace** R foot.	3	Slow	Arch
14	Step L foot **to the left** to face your partner.	4	Quick	Closed
15	Close R foot **to left foot**.	&	Quick	Closed
16-20	Execute steps 6-10 of cha cha basic.			

Step #13

Step #14

CHA CHA
Progressive Basic
-Man's Footwork-

Step	Description	Timing	Rhythmic Cue	Lead
1-5	Execute steps 1-5 of cha cha basic.			
6	Step R foot **to the right**.	1	Slow	R fingertips pull
7	Step L foot **forward**.	2	Slow	R hand heel push
8	**Replace** R foot.	3	Slow	R fingers pull and release
9	Step L foot **backward** (small step) passing right foot.	4	Quick	L hand hold pull
10	Step R foot **backward** (small step) passing left foot.	&	Quick	L hand hold pull
11	Step L foot **backward** (small step) passing right foot.	1	Slow	L hand hold pull
12	Step R foot **back**.	2	Slow	L hand hold pull
13	**Replace** L foot.	3	Slow	L hand hold push
14	Step R foot **forward** (small step) passing left foot.	4	Quick	L hand hold push
15	Step L foot **forward** (small step) passing right foot.	&	Quick	L hand hold push

(continued on page 154)

Step #6

Step #7

152

CHA CHA
Progressive Basic
-Woman's Footwork-

Step	Description	Timing	Rhythmic Cue	Position
1-5	Execute steps 1-5 of cha cha basic.			
6	Step L foot **to the left**.	1	Slow	Closed
7	Step R foot **back**.	2	Slow	Closed
8	**Replace** L foot.	3	Slow	Closed to open
9	Step R foot **forward** (small step) passing left foot.	4	Quick	Open, single hand hold
10	Step L foot **forward** (small step) passing right foot.	&	Quick	Open, single hand hold
11	Step R foot **forward** (small step) passing left foot.	1	Slow	Open, single hand hold
12	Step L foot **forward**.	2	Slow	Open, single hand hold
13	**Replace** R foot.	3	Slow	Open, single hand hold
14	Step L foot **backward** (small step) passing right foot.	4	Quick	Open, single hand hold
15	Step R foot **backward** (small step) passing left foot.	&	Quick	Open, single hand hold

(continued on page 155)

Step #8

Step #9

CHA CHA
Progressive Basic
-Man's Footwork, con't.-

Step	Description	Timing	Rhythmic Cue	Lead
16	Step R foot **forward** (small step) passing left foot.	1	Slow	L hand hold push
*	(Repeat steps 7-16 to continue progressive basic. Lead becomes visual.)			
17	Step L foot **forward**.	2	Slow	L hand hold push, R hand hold
18	**Replace** R foot.	3	Slow	R fingers pull
19	Step L foot **to the left**.	4	Quick	R hand palm push
20	Close R foot **to left foot**.	&	Quick	R hand palm push

Step #17

Step #18

CHA CHA
Progressive Basic
-Woman's Footwork, con't.-

Step	Description	Timing	Rhythmic Cue	Position
16	Step L foot **backward** (small step) passing right foot.	1	Slow	Open, single hand hold
*	(Repeat steps 7-16 to continue progressive basic).			
17	Step R foot **back**.	2	Slow	Closed
18	**Replace** L foot.	3	Slow	Closed
19	Step R foot **to the right**.	4	Quick	Closed
20	Close L foot **to right foot**.	&	Quick	Closed

Step #19

Step #20

CHA CHA
Chase Turns
-Man's Footwork-

Step	Description	Timing	Rhythmic Cue	Lead
1-16	Execute steps 1-16 of progressive basic.			
17	Step L foot **forward** pivoting 1/2 turn clockwise (right).	2	Slow	Visual
18	**Replace** R foot.	3	Slow	Visual
19	Step L foot **forward** (small step).	4	Quick	Visual
20	Step R foot **forward** (small step).	&	Quick	Visual
21	Step L foot **forward** (small step).	1	Slow	Visual
22	Step R foot **forward** pivoting 1/2 turn counter-clockwise (left).	2	Slow	Visual
23	**Replace** L foot.	3	Slow	Visual
24	Step R foot **forward** (small step).	4	Quick	Visual
25	Step L foot **forward** (small step).	&	Quick	Visual

(continued on page 158)

Step #17

Step #18

CHA CHA
Chase Turns
-Woman's Footwork-

Step	Description	Timing	Rhythmic Cue	Position
1-16	Execute steps 1-16 of progressive basic.			
17	Step R foot **back**.	2	Slow	Open
18	**Replace** L foot.	3	Slow	Open
19	Step R foot **forward** (small step).	4	Quick	Open
20	Step L foot **forward** (small step).	&	Quick	Open
21	Step R foot **forward** (small step).	1	Slow	Open
22	Step L foot **forward** pivoting 1/2 turn clockwise (right).	2	Slow	Open
23	**Replace** R foot.	3	Slow	Open
24	Step L foot **forward** (small step).	4	Quick	Open
25	Step R foot **forward** (small step).	&	Quick	Open

(continued on page 159)

Step #22

Step #23

Step	Description	Timing	Rhythmic Cue	Lead
26	Step R foot **forward** (small step).	1	Slow	Visual
	Repeat steps 17-26 to continue chase.			
27	Step L foot **forward**.	2	Slow	Visual
28	**Replace** R foot.	3	Slow	Visual
29	Step L foot **backward** (small step).	4	Quick	Visual
30	Step R foot **backward** (small step).	&	Quick	Visual
31	Step L foot **backward** (small step).	1	Slow	Visual
32	Step R foot **back**.	2	Slow	L hand hold
33	**Replace** L foot.	3	Slow	R hand heel push
34	Step R foot **to the right**.	4	Quick	R fingertips pull
35	Close L foot **to right foot**.	&	Quick	R fingertips pull
36-40	Execute steps 6-10 of cha cha basic.			

Step #31

Step #32

Step	Description	Timing	Rhythmic Cue	Position
26	Step L foot **forward** (small step).	1	Slow	Open
27	Step R foot **forward** pivoting 1/2 turn counter-clockwise (left).	2	Slow	Open
28	**Replace** L foot.	3	Slow	Open
29	Step R foot **forward** (small step).	4	Quick	Open
30	Step L foot **forward** (small step).	&	Quick	Open
31	Step R foot **forward** (small step).	1	Slow	Open

(Repeat steps 22-31 until your partner stops turning. You will see his face instead of his back).

Step	Description	Timing	Rhythmic Cue	Position
32	Step L foot **forward**.	2	Slow	Open
33	**Replace** R foot.	3	Slow	Closed
34	Step L foot **to the left**.	4	Quick	Closed
35	Close R foot **to left foot**.	&	Quick	Closed
36-40	Execute steps 6-10 of cha cha basic.			

Step #33

Step #34

CHA CHA
Full Turn
-Man's Footwork-

Step	Description	Timing	Rhythmic Cue	Lead
1-16	Execute steps 1-16 of progressive basic.			
17	Step L foot **forward** pivoting 1/2 turn clockwise (right).	2	Slow	Visual
18	**Replace** R foot pivoting 1/2 turn clockwise.	3	Slow	Visual
19	Step L foot **backward** (small step).	4	Quick	Visual
20	Step R foot **backward** (small step).	&	Quick	Visual
21	Step L foot **backward** (small step).	1	Slow	Visual
22	Step R foot **back**.	2	Slow	Visual
23	**Replace** L foot.	3	Slow	Visual
24	Step R foot **forward** (small step).	4	Quick	Visual
25	Step L foot **forward** (small step).	&	Quick	Visual
26	Step R foot **forward** (small step).	1	Slow	Visual

Note: To continue full turns repeat steps 17-26 or return to progressive basic or basic step.

Step #17

Step #18

CHA CHA
Full Turn
-Woman's Footwork-

Step	Description	Timing	Rhythmic Cue	Position
1-16	Execute steps 1-16 of progressive basic.			
17	Step R foot **back**.	2	Slow	Open
18	**Replace** L foot.	3	Slow	Open
19	Step R foot **forward** (small step).	4	Quick	Open
20	Step L foot **forward** (small step).	&	Quick	Open
21	Step R foot **forward** (small step).	1	Slow	Open
22	Step L foot **forward** pivoting 1/2 turn clockwise (right).	2	Slow	Open
23	**Replace** R foot pivoting 1/2 turn clockwise.	3	Slow	Open
24	Step L foot **backward** (small step).	4	Quick	Open
25	Step R foot **backward** (small step).	&	Quick	Open
26	Step L foot **backward** (small step).	1	Slow	Open

Note: To continue full turns repeat steps 17-26 or return to progressive basic or basic step.

Step #19

Step #23

MUSIC FOR CHA CHA

Isle of Capri

Tea for Two Cha Cha

Never on Sunday

Whatever Lola Wants

Black Magic Woman

Oye Como Va

Poco Pelo

Never Again

Tropical Cha Cha

Me Gusto el Cha Cha

Sweet and Gentle

MAMBO

MAMBO

HISTORY

In the late 1940s Havana, Cuba, was a popular holiday resort for American tourists. American and Latin bands that entertained in the casinos and night clubs developed a new rhythm combining American jazz and Cuban rhumba called the mambo (name borrowed from a priestess of African religion). A dance was developed to fit the music, characterized by an accent on the off beat (second beat of the measure) and the Cuban hip motion.

RHYTHMICAL ANALYSIS

The mambo is written in 4/4 time with the accent on the second beat of the measure; the first beat of the measure is held. The rhythm pattern, beginning on step two, is quick, quick, slow. Tempo of the music is 40-51 measures per minute, 160-204 beats per minute.

STYLING

The mambo is a spot dance that utilizes closed and open positions. Toes are turned slightly outward, steps are very small and fast and are taken on flat feet, rolling the weight from inside to outside. The knees are kept soft and weight is shifted after the step is taken, utilizing the Cuban hip motion. The man's left arm and the woman's right arm are bent at approximately a right angle, with little or no space between the forearms.

MAMBO

* 1. Mambo Basic, Turning Left

* 2. Crossover Breaks

* 3. Walk Around Turn

   4. Parallel Breaks

* 5. Open Break with Underarm (Arch) Turn

* 6. Progressive Basic

* 7. Chase Turns

* 8. Full Turn

MAMBO BASIC ANALYSIS

Man									
		Forward	Back	Side			Back	Forward	Side
	1	2	3	4		1	2	3	4
		--	--	- - - -			--	--	- - - -
		Quick	Quick	Slow			Quick	Quick	Slow
Woman		Back	Forward	Side			Forward	Back	Side

MAMBO
Mambo Basic
-Man's Footwork-

Step	Description	Timing	Rhythmic Cue	Lead
1	Hold.	1		R hand hold
2	Step L foot **forward** (rock step).	2	Quick	R hand heel push
3	**Replace** R foot.	3	Quick	R fingers pull
4	Step L foot **to the left**.	4	Slow	R hand palm push
5	Hold.	1		R hand hold
6	Step R foot **back** (rock step).	2	Quick	R fingers pull
7	**Replace** L foot.	3	Quick	R hand heel push
8	Step R foot **to the right**.	4	Slow	R fingertips pull

Note: To execute mambo basic turning left, turn left foot outward beginning 1/4 turn on step 2. Complete 1/4 turn to the left on step 3.

Step #2

Step #3

MAMBO
Mambo Basic
-Woman's Footwork-

Step	Description	Timing	Rhythmic Cue	Position
1	Hold.	1		Closed
2	Step R foot **back** (rock step).	2	Quick	Closed
3	**Replace** L foot.	3	Quick	Closed
4	Step R foot **to the right**.	4	Slow	Closed
5	Hold.	1		Closed
6	Step L foot **forward** (rock step).	2	Quick	Closed
7	**Replace** R foot.	3	Quick	Closed
8	Step L foot **to the left**.	4	Slow	Closed

Note: To execute mambo basic turning left, turn right foot inward beginning 1/4 turn on step 2. Complete 1/4 turn to the left on step 3.

Step #4

Step #6

MAMBO
Crossover Breaks
-Man's Footwork-

Step	Description	Timing	Rhythmic Cue	Lead
1-8	Execute steps 1-8 of mambo basic. Turn right foot outward on step 8 beginning 1/4 turn.			
9	Hold (no step).	1		R hand hold
10	Step L foot **across right foot**.	2	Quick	L hand hold moves inward R hand hold release
11	**Replace** R foot.	3	Quick	L hand hold pull
12	Step L foot **to the left** (toe outward) turning 1/4 turn left.	4	Slow	Double hand hold
13	Hold (no step).	1		Double hand hold
14	Step R foot **across left foot**.	2	Quick	R hand hold moves inward L hand hold release
15	**Replace** L foot.	3	Quick	R hand hold pull
16	Step R foot **to the right** (toe outward) turning 1/4 turn right (toe points forward to return to basic step).	4	Slow	Double hand hold
17-24	Repeat steps 9-16.			
25	Hold (no step).	1		Double hand hold
26	Step L foot **forward**.	2	Quick	L & R hand hold push
27	**Replace** R foot.	3	Quick	L & R hand hold pull
28	Step L foot **to the left**.	4	Slow	L & R hand hold

Step #8

Step #10

MAMBO
Crossover Breaks
-Woman's Footwork-

Step	Description	Timing	Rhythmic Cue	Position
1-8	Execute steps 1-8 of mambo basic. Turn left foot outward on step 8 beginning 1/4 turn.			
9	Hold (no step).	1		Closed
10	Step R foot **across left foot**.	2	Quick	Crossover
11	**Replace** L foot.	3	Quick	Crossover
12	Step R foot **to the right** (toe outward) turning 1/4 turn right.	4	Slow	Double hand hold
13	Hold (no step).	1		Double hand hold
14	Step L foot **across right foot**.	2	Quick	Crossover
15	**Replace** R foot.	3	Quick	Crossover
16	Step L foot **to the left** (toe outward) turning 1/4 turn left (toe points forward to return to basic step).	4	Slow	Double hand hold
17-24	Repeat steps 9-16.			
25	Hold (no step).	1		Double hand hold
26	Step R foot **back**.	2	Quick	Double hand hold
27	**Replace** L foot.	3	Quick	Double hand hold
28	Step R foot **to the right**.	4	Slow	Closed

Step #12

Step #14

MAMBO
Walk Around Turn
-Man's Footwork-

Note: Walk around turn replaces steps 21-24 of crossover breaks. It usually replaces the 4th crossover. As you begin the turn place your right arm behind your back instead of taking a double hand hold. (A right hand lead may be executed after taking a double hand hold.)

Step	Description	Timing	Rhythmic Cue	Lead
1-20	Execute steps 1-20 of crossover break.			
21	Hold (no step).	1		Place L palm to partners right palm
22	Step R foot **across left foot** pivoting 1/2 turn left.	2	Quick	L hand palm push
23	**Replace** L foot completing a full turn to face your partner.	3	Quick	Visual
24	Step R foot **to the right**.	4	Slow	Retake closed position
25-28	Execute steps 1-4 of mambo basic.			

Step #21

Step #22

MAMBO
Walk Around Turn
-Woman's Footwork-

Note: Walk around turn replaces steps 21-24 of crossover breaks. It usually replaces the 4th crossover. As you begin the turn place your left arm behind your back instead of taking a double hand hold.

Step	Description	Timing	Rhythmic Cue	Position
1-20	Execute steps 1-20 of crossover break.			
21	Hold (no step).	1		Double hand hold
22	Step L foot **across right foot** pivoting 1/2 turn right.	2	Quick	Crossover
23	**Replace** R foot completing a full turn to face your partner.	3	Quick	Open
24	Step L foot **to the left**.	4	Slow	Closed
25-28	Execute steps 1-4 of mambo basic.			

Step #23

Step #24

MAMBO
Parallel Breaks
-Man's Footwork-

Step	Description	Timing	Rhythmic Cue	Lead
1-8	Execute steps 1-8 of mambo basic. Turn right foot outward on step 8.			
9	Hold.	1		
10	Step L foot **across right foot** (turning 1/8 turn right).	2	Quick	R hand CW turn, L hand hold push
11	**Replace** R foot.	3	Quick	R hand CCW turn, L hand hold pull
12	Step L foot **to the left** (toe outward).	4	Slow	R hand CCW turn, L hand hold pull
13	Hold.	1		R hand hold
14	Step R foot **across left foot** (turning 1/4 turn left).	2	Quick	R hand CCW turn
15	**Replace** R foot.	3	Quick	R hand CW turn
*	Repeat steps 8-15 to continue parallel breaks. Step 10 will become a 1/4 turn.			
16	Step R foot **to the right**.	4	Slow	R hand CW turn

Step #10

Step #11

Step	Description	Timing	Rhythmic Cue	Position
1-8	Execute steps 1-8 of mambo basic. Turn left foot inward on step 8.			
9	Hold.	1		
10	Step R foot **behind left foot** in left parallel position.	2	Quick	Left parallel
11	**Replace** L foot.	3	Quick	Left parallel to closed
12	Step R foot **to the right** (toe inward).	4	Slow	Closed
13	Hold.	1		Closed
14	Step L foot **behind right foot** in right parallel position.	2	Quick	Right parallel
15	**Replace** R foot.	3	Quick	Right parallel to closed
*	Repeat steps 8-15 to continue parallel breaks.			
16	Step L foot **to the left**.	4	Slow	Closed

Step #14

Step #15

MAMBO
Open Break with Arch Turn
-Man's Footwork-

Precede with a basic step.

Step	Description	Timing	Rhythmic Cue	Lead
1	Hold (no step).	1		L & R hand hold
2	Step L foot **back** as right arm extends forward at elbow level.	2	Quick	L hand hold push, R hand hold release
3	**Replace** R foot.	3	Quick	L hand hold pull
4	Step L foot **diagonally to the left** in line with left foot.	4	Slow	L hand hold
5	Hold (no step).	1		L hand hold
6	Step R foot **back** leading your partner into an arch turn.	2	Quick	L hand hold extends up and out
7	**Replace** L foot.	3	Quick	L hand hold encircles CW
8	Step R foot **diagonally to the right** in line with left foot.	4	Slow	L hand hold lowers

Step #2

Step #6

174

MAMBO
Open Break with Arch Turn
-Woman's Footwork-

Precede with a basic step.

Step	Description	Timing	Rhythmic Cue	Position
1	Hold (no step).	1		Closed
2	Step R foot **back**.	2	Quick	Open, single hand hold
3	**Replace** L foot.	3	Quick	Open, single hand hold
4	Step R foot **diagonally to the right** in line with left foot with toe turned out.	4	Slow	Open, single hand hold
5	Hold (no step).	1		Open, single hand hold
6	Step L foot **across right foot** pivoting 1/2 turn right.	2	Quick	Arch
7	**Replace** R foot.	3	Quick	Arch
8	Step L foot **to the left** in line with right foot to face your partner.	4	Slow	Closed

Step #7

Step #8

MAMBO
Progressive Basic
-Man's Footwork-

Step	Description	Timing	Rhythmic Cue	Lead
1-7	Execute steps 1-7 of mambo basic.			
8	Step R foot **forward** passing left foot.	4	Slow	R hand heel push
9	Hold (no step).	1		L & R hand hold
10	Step L foot **forward** passing left foot.	2	Quick	L hand heel push
11	**Replace** R foot.	3	Quick	R fingers pull
12	Step L foot **backward** passing right foot.	4	Slow	Visual
13-20	Repeat steps 5-12 in open position.			
21	Hold (no step).	1		L & R hand hold
22	Step R foot **backward**.	2	Quick	R fingers pull
23	**Replace** L foot.	3	Quick	R hand heel push
24	Step R foot **to the right**.	4	Slow	R fingertips pull

Step #10

Step #11

MAMBO
Progressive Basic
-Woman's Footwork-

Step	Description	Timing	Rhythmic Cue	Position
1-7	Execute steps 1-7 of mambo basic.			
8	Step L foot **backward** passing right foot.	4	Slow	Closed
9	Hold (no step).	1		Closed
10	Step R foot **backward** passing left foot.	2	Quick	Closed
11	**Replace** L foot.	3	Quick	Closed into open
12	Step R foot **forward** passing left foot.	4	Slow	Open
13-20	Repeat steps 5-12.			
21	Hold (no step).	1		Closed
22	Step L foot **forward**.	2	Quick	Closed
23	**Replace** R foot.	3	Quick	Closed
24	Step L foot **to the left**.	4	Slow	Closed

Step #12

Step #14

MAMBO
Chase Turns
-Man's Footwork-

Execute steps 1-16 of progressive basic.

Step	Description	Timing	Rhythmic Cue	Lead
17	Hold.	1		Visual
18	Step L foot **forward** pivoting 1/2 turn clockwise (right).	2	Quick	Visual
19	**Replace** R foot.	3	Quick	Visual
20	Step L foot **forward** passing right foot.	4	Slow	Visual
21	Hold.	1		Visual
22	Step R foot **forward** pivoting 1/2 turn counter-clockwise (left).	2	Quick	Visual
23	**Replace** L foot.	3	Quick	Visual
24	Step R foot **forward** passing left foot.	4	Slow	Visual
*	Repeat chase turns, return to basic step or execute full turn (page 180).			

Step #18

Step #19

MAMBO
Chase Turns
-Woman's Footwork-

Precede with progressive basic.

Step	Description	Timing	Rhythmic Cue	Position
17	Hold.	1		Open
18	Step R foot **back**.	2	Quick	Open
19	**Replace** L foot.	3	Quick	Open
20	Step R foot **forward** passing left foot.	4	Slow	Open
21	Hold.	1		Open
22	Step L foot **forward** pivoting 1/2 turn counter-clockwise (left).	2	Quick	Open
23	**Replace** R foot.	3	Quick	Open
24	Step L foot **forward** passing right foot.	4	Slow	Open
25	Hold.	1		Open
26	Step R foot **forward** pivoting 1/2 turn counter-clockwise (left).	2	Quick	Open
27	**Replace** L foot.	3	Quick	Open
28	Step R foot **forward** passing left foot.	4	Slow	Open

* Repeat chase turns, return to basic step or execute full turn (page 181).

Step #22

Step #23

MAMBO
Full Turn
-Man's Footwork-

Execute steps 1-16 of progressive basic or steps 1-24 of chase turns.

Step	Description	Timing	Rhythmic Cue	Lead
1	Hold.	1		Visual
2	Step L foot **forward** pivoting 1/2 turn clockwise (right).	2	Quick	Visual
3	**Replace** R pivoting 1/2 turn clockwise (right).	3	Quick	Visual
4	Step L foot **backward**.	4	Slow	Visual
5	Hold.	1		Visual
6	Step R foot **backward**.	2	Quick	Visual
7	**Replace** L foot.	3	Quick	Visual
8	Step R foot **forward**.	4	Slow	Visual

*   Repeat full turn or return to basic step.

Step #2

Step #3

MAMBO
Full Turn
-Woman's Footwork-

Precede with progressive basic or chase turns.

Step	Description	Timing	Rhythmic Cue	Position
1	Hold.	1		Open
2	Step R foot **back**.	2	Quick	Open
3	**Replace** L foot.	3	Quick	Open
4	Step R foot **forward** passing left foot.	4	Slow	Open
5	Hold.	1		Open
6	Step L foot **forward** pivoting 1/2 turn clockwise (right).	2	Quick	Open
7	**Replace** R foot pivoting 1/2 turn clockwise (right).	3	Quick	Open
8	Step L foot **backward** (small step).	4	Slow	Open
9	Hold.	1		Open
10	Step R foot **back**.	2	Quick	Open
11	**Replace** L foot.	3	Quick	Open
12	Step R foot **forward** passing left foot.	4	Slow	Open
*	Repeat full turn or return to basic step.			

Step #4

Step #6

MUSIC FOR MAMBO

Tequila

The Ingenue Mambo

Senora

Mambo Jambo

Timbales Mambo

El Guapo

The Panther Mambo

The Hat Mambo

Mambo Loco

SAMBA

SAMBA

HISTORY

Inherited from black African culture, the Brazilians of African descent celebrated the Lenten season by dancing in the streets. As parades moved through the streets "semba" was a command to break away and perform improvised dances. Over the years, "semba" has evolved into "samba". During the 20s and 30s the improvised rhythms were standardized and moved into closed dance positions suitable for the ballrooms of the United States. The bouncy rhythm and swaying bodies are the principal characteristics of this exuberant dance. The music and dance of the samba remain the theme for Carnival in Rio de Janerio and Mardi Gras in New Orleans.

RHYTHMICAL ANALYSIS

Music for the samba is written in 2/4 time with the first two steps receiving 3/4 and 1/4 beat respectively. The third steps gets a full beat which results in a bouncy style movement. Rhythm pattern is cued "1 and ah two." Tempo of the music is 48-58 measures per minute, 96-116 beats per minute.

STYLING

Samba has a unique style characterized by the body swaying (pendular movement) in opposition to the feet. Knees remain relaxed, ankles are flexible and weight is taken on the balls of the feet. Movement is initiated in the feet and the feet and legs swing forward and backward in a larger arc than the upper body. The samba is executed in a small space, a spot dance. Partners sometimes break away, moving around each other with arms moving freely in opposition to their bodies.

SAMBA

* 1. Samba Basic, Left Box Turn

* 2. Balancetes

* 3. Underarm (Arch) Turn

* 4. Copacabana

  5. Botofogo

  6. Two-Way Compaso

SAMBA BASIC ANALYSIS

Man	Forward 1+ (3/4)	Side ah (1/4)	Close 2	Back 1+ (3/4)	Side ah (1/4)	Close 2
	- - -	-	- - - -	- - -	-	- - - -
	Quick	ah	Slow	Quick	ah	Slow
Woman	Back	Side	Close	Forward	Side	Close

185

SAMBA
Basic Step
-Man's Footwork-

Step	Description	Timing	Rhythmic Cue	Lead
1	Step L foot **forward**.	3/4	Quick	R hand heel push
2	Step R foot **forward** slightly **to the right** in line with left foot. Take partial weight on the ball of right foot.	1/4	ah	R fingertips pull
3	Close (pull) L foot **to right foot**.	2	Slow	R hand hold
4	Step R foot **backward**.	3/4	Quick	R fingers pull
5	Step L foot **backward** slightly **to the left** in line with right foot. Take partial weight on the ball of left foot.	1/4	ah	R hand palm push
6	Close (pull) R foot **to left foot**.	2	Slow	R hand hold

Step #1

Step #2

SAMBA
Basic Step
-Woman's Footwork-

Step	Description	Timing	Rhythmic Cue	Position
1	Step R foot **backward**.	3/4	Quick	Closed
2	Step L foot **backward** slightly **to the left** in line with right foot. Take partial weight on the ball of left foot.	1/4	ah	Closed
3	Close (pull) R foot **to left foot**.	2	Slow	Closed
4	Step L foot **forward**.	3/4	Quick	Closed
5	Step R foot **forward** slightly **to the right** in line with left foot. Take partial weight on the ball of right foot.	1/4	ah	Closed
6	Close (pull) L foot **to right foot**.	2	Slow	Closed

Step #3

Step #4

SAMBA
Left Box Turn
-Man's Footwork-

Step	Description	Timing	Rhythmic Cue	Lead
1	Step L foot **forward** turning toe outward beginning 1/4 turn left.	3/4	Quick	R hand palm push
2	Step R foot **to the right** completing turn.	1/4	ah	R fingertips pull
3	Close L foot **to right foot**.	2	Slow	R hand hold
4	Step R foot **backward** turning toe inward beginning 1/4 turn left.	3/4	Quick	R fingers pull
5	Step L foot **to the left** completing turn.	1/4	ah	R hand palm push
6	Close R foot **to left foot**.	2	Slow	R hand hold

Note: Repeat steps 1-6 to complete left box turn (counter-clockwise).

Step #1

Step #2

SAMBA
Left Box Turn
-Woman's Footwork-

Step	Description	Timing	Rhythmic Cue	Position
1	Step R foot **backward** turning toe inward beginning 1/4 turn left.	3/4	Quick	Closed
2	Step L foot **to the left** completing turn.	1/4	ah	Closed
3	Close R foot **to left foot**.	2	Slow	Closed
4	Step L foot **forward** turning toe outward beginning 1/4 turn left.	3/4	Quick	Closed
5	Step R foot **to the right** completing turn.	1/4	ah	Closed
6	Close L foot **to right foot**.	2	Slow	Closed

Note: Repeat steps 1-6 to complete left box turn (counter-clockwise).

Step #3

Step #4

SAMBA
Balancetes
-Man's Footwork-

Step	Description	Timing	Rhythmic Cue	Lead
1	Step L foot **to the left**.	3/4	Quick	R hand palm push
2	Step R foot **to the left** in 5th position (feet are at a right angle with right toe at left heel).	1/4	ah	R hand CCW turn
3	Pull L foot **slightly back**.	2	Slow	R hand CW turn
4	Step R foot **to the right**.	3/4	Quick	R fingertips pull
5	Step L foot **to the right** in 5th position (feet are at a right angle with left toe to right heel).	1/4	ah	R hand CW turn
6	Pull R foot **slightly back**.	2	Slow	R hand CCW turn

Note: Return to left box turn.

Step #1

Step #2

SAMBA
Balancetes
-Woman's Footwork-

Step	Description	Timing	Rhythmic Cue	Position
1	Step R foot **to the right**.	3/4	Quick	Closed
2	Step L foot **to the right** in 5th position (feet are at a right angle with left toe at right heel).	1/4	ah	Fifth position
3	Pull R foot **slightly back**.	2	Slow	Fifth position
4	Step L foot **to the left**.	3/4	Quick	Closed
5	Step R foot **to the left** in 5th position (feet are at a right angle with right toe to left heel).	1/4	ah	Fifth position
6	Pull L foot **slightly back**.	2	Slow	Fifth position

Step #4

Step #5

SAMBA
Arch Turn
-Man's Footwork-

Precede with balancete.

Step	Description	Timing	Rhythmic Cue	Lead
1	Step L foot **to the left**.	3/4	Quick	L hand hold extends up and out
2	Step R foot **to the left** in 5th position leading partner into arch turn.	1/4	ah	L hand hold encircles CW
3	Pull L foot **slightly back**.	2	Slow	Left hand hold lowers
4	Step R foot **to the right**.	3/4	Quick	L & R hand hold
5	Step L foot **to the right** in 5th position.	1/4	ah	R hand CW turn
6	Pull R foot **slightly back**.	2	Slow	R hand CCW turn
*	Return to left box turn.			

Step #1

Step #2

SAMBA
Arch Turn
-Woman's Footwork-

Precede with balancete.

Step	Description	Timing	Rhythmic Cue	Position
1	Step R foot **to the right** turning toe out.	3/4	Quick	Arch
2	Step L foot **across right foot** pivoting 1/2 turn right.	1/4	ah	Arch
3	**Replace** R foot facing your partner.	2	Slow	Closed
4	Step L foot **to the left**.	3/4	Quick	Closed
5	Step R foot **to the left** in 5th position.	1/4	ah	Closed
6	Pull L foot **slightly back**.	2	Slow	Closed

Step #3

Step #4

SAMBA
Copacabana
— Man's Footwork —

Precede with balancetes (steps 1-6).

Step	Description	Timing	Rhythmic Cue	Lead
1	Step L foot **forward** in promenade position.	3/4	Quick	R hand palm push
2	Step R foot slightly **backward** taking partial weight on the ball of foot.	1/4	ah	L & R hand hold
3	Pull L foot slightly **backward** taking the weight.	2	Slow	R hand hold pull
4	Step R foot **forward** passing left foot in promenade position.	3/4	Quick	R hand palm push
5	Step L foot slighly **backward** taking partial weight on the ball of foot.	1/4	ah	L & R hand hold
6	Pull R foot slightly **backward** taking the weight.	2	Slow	R hand hold pull
7-9	Repeat steps 1-3.			
10	Step R foot **forward** passing left foot turning toe outward.	3/4	Quick	R hand palm push
11	Step L foot **to the side** (partial weight) to face your partner.	1/4	ah	R hand CCW turn
12	Close (pull) R foot **to left foot**.	2	Slow	L & R hand hold

Step #1

Step #2

Copacabana
— Woman's Footwork —

Precede with balancetes (steps 1-6).

Step	Description	Timing	Rhythmic Cue	Position
1	Step R foot **forward**.	3/4	Quick	Promenade
2	Step L foot slightly **backward** taking partial weight on the ball of feet.	1/4	ah	Promenade
3	Pull R foot slightly **backward** taking the weight.	2	Slow	Promenade
4	Step L foot **forward** passing right foot.	3/4	Quick	Promenade
5	Step R foot slighly **backward** taking partial weight on the ball of foot.	1/4	ah	Promenade
6	Pull L foot slightly **backward** taking the weight.	2	Slow	Promenade
7-9	Repeat steps 1-3.			
10	Step L foot **forward** passing right foot turning toe outward.	3/4	Quick	Promenade to closed
11	Step R foot **to the side** (partial weight) to face your partner.	1/4	ah	Closed
12	Close (pull) L foot **to right foot**.	2	Slow	Closed

Step #3

Step #4

SAMBA
Botofogo
— Man's Footwork —

Step	Description	Timing	Rhythmic Cue	Lead
1	Step L foot **forward**.	3/4	Quick	R hand heel push
2	Step R foot **to the right** (partial weight) with toe inward.	1/4	ah	R fingers pull and CW turn
3	Close (pull) L foot **toward right foot** in promenade position.	2	Slow	L & R hand hold
4	Step R foot **forward** passing left foot turning toe outward.	3/4	Quick	R hand palm push
5	Step L foot **to the side** (partial weight) to face your partner).	1/4	ah	R hand CCW turn
6	Close (pull) R foot **to left foot**.	2	Slow	L & R hand hold

Step #1

Step #2

SAMBA
Botofogo
— Woman's Footwork —

Step	Description	Timing	Rhythmic Cue	Position
1	Step R foot **backward**.	3/4	Quick	Closed
2	Step L foot **to the left** (partial weight) with toe inward.	1/4	ah	Closed to promenade
3	Close (pull) R foot **toward left foot**.	2	Slow	Promenade
4	Step L foot **forward** passing right foot turning toe outward.	3/4	Quick	Promenade
5	Step R foot **to the side** (partial weight) to face your partner.	1/4	ah	Promenade to closed
6	Close (pull) L foot **to right foot**.	2	Slow	Closed

Step #4

Step #5

SAMBA
Two-Way Compaso
— Man's Footwork —

Step	Description	Timing	Rhythmic Cue	Lead
1	Step L foot **forward**.	1	Slow	R hand heel push
2	Step R foot **to the right** in line with left foot.	ah	Quick	R fingertips pull
3	Close (pull) L foot **to right foot**.	2	Slow	L & R hand hold
4	Step R foot **to the right**.	ah	Quick	R fingertips pull
5	Close (pull) L foot **to right foot**.	3	Slow	L & R hand hold
6	Step R foot **to the right**.	ah	Quick	R fingertips pull
7	Close (pull) L foot **to right foot**.	4	Slow	L & R hand hold
8	Step R foot **backward**.	5	Slow	R fingers pull
9	Step L foot **to the left** in line with right foot.	ah	Quick	R hand palm push
10	Close (pull) R foot **to left foot**.	6	Slow	L & R hand hold
11	Step L foot **to the left**.	ah	Quick	R hand palm push
12	Close (pull) R foot **to left foot**.	7	Slow	L & R hand hold
13	Step L foot **to the left**.	ah	Quick	R hand palm push
14	Close (pull) R foot **to left foot**.	8	Slow	L & R hand hold

Step #1

Step #2

SAMBA
Two-Way Compaso
— *Woman's Footwork* —

Step	Description	Timing	Rhythmic Cue	Position
1	Step R foot **backward**.	1	Slow	Closed
2	Step L foot **to the left** in line with right foot.	ah	Quick	Closed
3	Close (pull) R foot **to left foot**.	2	Slow	Closed
4	Step L foot **to the left**.	ah	Quick	Closed
5	Close (pull) R foot **to left foot**.	3	Slow	Closed
6	Step L foot **to the left**.	ah	Quick	Closed
7	Close (pull) R foot **to left foot**.	4	Slow	Closed
8	Step L foot **forward**.	5	Slow	Closed
9	Step R foot **to the right** in line with left foot.	ah	Quick	Closed
10	Close (pull) L foot **to right foot**.	6	Slow	Closed
11	Step R foot **to the right**.	ah	Quick	Closed
12	Close (pull) L foot **to right foot**.	7	Slow	Closed
13	Step R foot **to the right**.	ah	Quick	Closed
14	Close (pull) L foot **to right foot**.	8	Slow	Closed

Step #3

Step #4

MUSIC FOR SAMBA

Copacabana

Brazil

Cuando, Cuando, Cuando

El Bimbo

Marina

Tico, Tico

La Bamba

Assambraco

Viv Meu Samba

Samba de Orfeo

MERENGUE

MERENGUE

HISTORY

The merengue was developed in the Caribbean islands as a natural accompaniment to the Calypso rhythms played by the native musicians. Danced alone it is spontaneous and creative, moving around a partner with no particular pattern. Danced with a partner it can utilize variations from the rhumba or move in a sideward direction. It uses a step-close pattern, or one-step, and is the easiest of the Latin dances to execute.

RHYTHMICAL ANALYSIS

The merengue is written in 2/4 time with each step getting an even beat. Tempo of the music is 29-32 measures per minute, 116-128 beats per minute.

STYLING

The merengue uses the Cuban hip motion ranging from smooth and controlled to a staccato action. It's basic step moves to the side and the first beat of the measure is accented. There is very little movement of the upper body. Partners may utilize a subtle hip action and stately position or break away into more relaxed creative moves with a natural response to the music.

MERENGUE

1. Merengue Basic

2. Stair Steps

3. Forward and Backward Walks

4. Promenade

5. Left Rock Turn

6. Separation into Wringer

BASIC STEP ANALYSIS

Man	Side	Close	Side	Close	
	1	2	1	2	
	- -	- -	- -	- -	
Woman	Side	Close	Side	Close	

MERENGUE
Basic Step
-Man's Footwork-

Step	Description	Timing	Lead
1	Place L foot **to the left** (partial weight).	1	R hand push
2	Close R foot **to left foot** (partial weight) shifting weight to left foot.	2	R hand pressure

Note: Cuban motion is analyzed in the description of the basic step only.

Stair Steps
-Man's Footwork-

Step	Description	Timing	Lead
1	Step L foot **to the left**.	1	R hand palm push
2	Close R foot **to left foot**.	2	R hand pressure
3	Step L foot **forward**.	1	R hand heel push
4	Close R foot **to left foot**.	2	R hand pressure

Basic Step #1

Basic Step #2

MERENGUE
Basic Step
-Woman's Footwork-

Step	Description	Timing	Position
1	Step R foot **to the right** (partial weight).	1	Closed
2	Close L foot **to right foot** (partial weight) shifting weight to right foot.	2	Closed

Note: Cuban motion is analyzed in the description of the basic step only.

Stair Steps
-Woman's Footwork-

Step	Description	Timing	Position
1	Step R foot **to the right**.	1	Closed
2	Close L foot **to right foot**.	2	Closed
3	Step R foot **backward**.	1	Closed
4	Close L foot **to right foot**.	2	Closed

Stair Step #3

Stair Step #4

MERENGUE
Forward and Backward Walks
-Man's Footwork-

Step	Description	Timing	Lead
	• Forward Walks		
1	Step L foot **forward**.	1	R hand heel push
2	Step R foot **forward** passing left foot.	2	R hand heel push
3	Step L foot **forward** passing right foot.	1	R hand heel push
4	Close R foot **to left foot**.	2	R hand hold
	• Backward Walks		
5	Step L foot **backward**.	1	R fingers pull
6	Step R foot **backward** passing left foot.	2	R fingers pull
7	Step L foot **backward** passing right foot.	1	R fingers pull
8	Close R foot **to left foot**.	2	R hand hold

Step #1

Step #2

MERENGUE
Forward and Backward Walks
-Woman's Footwork-

Step	Description	Timing	Position
	• **Forward Walks**		
1	Step R foot **backward**.	1	Closed
2	Step L foot **backward** passing right foot.	2	Closed
3	Step R foot **backward** passing left foot.	1	Closed
4	Close L foot **to right foot**.	2	Closed
	• **Backward Walks**		
5	Step R foot **forward**.	1	Closed
6	Step L foot **forward** passing right foot.	2	Closed
7	Step R foot **forward** passing left foot.	1	Closed
8	Close L foot **to right foot**.	2	Closed

Step #5

Step #6

MERENGUE
Promenade
-Man's Footwork-

Precede with merengue basic.

Step	Description	Timing	Lead
1	Step L foot **to the left** (toe outward) in promenade position.	1	R hand CW turn
2	Step R foot **forward** passing left foot.	2	R hand palm push
3	Step L foot **to the left** to face your partner.	1	R hand CCW turn
4	Close R foot **to left foot**.	2	R hand hold

Left Rock Turn
-Man's Footwork-

Step	Description	Timing	Lead
1	Step L foot **forward**.	1	R hand heel push
2	**Replace** R foot (toe inward) beginning 1/4 turn counter-clockwise.	2	R fingers pull
3	Step L foot **to the left** completing 1/4 turn left.	1	R hand push
4	Close R foot **to left foot**.	2	R hand hold

Promenade Step #1

Promenade Step #2

MERENGUE
Promenade
-Woman's Footwork-

Precede with merengue basic.

Step	Description	Timing	Position
1	Step R foot **to the right** (toe outward).	1	Closed into promenade
2	Step L foot **forward** passing right foot.	2	Promenade
3	Step R foot **to the right** to face your partner.	1	Promenade
4	Close L foot **to right foot**.	2	Promenade into closed

Left Rock Turn
-Woman's Footwork-

Step	Description	Timing	Position
1	Step R foot **backward**.	1	Closed
2	**Replace** L foot (toe outward) beginning 1/4 turn left.	2	Closed
3	Step R foot **to the right** completing 1/4 turn left.	1	Closed
4	Close L foot **to right foot**.	2	Closed

Left Rock Turn Step #1

Left Rock Turn Step #2

MERENGUE
Separation into Wringer
-Man's Footwork-

Step	Description	Timing	Lead
1	Step L foot **backward** beginning separation.	1	L hand hold push, R hand hold release
2	Step R foot **backward**.	2	L hand hold push
3	Step L foot **backward** taking double hand hold.	1	L & R hand holds
4	Close R foot **to left foot**.	2	L & R hand holds
5	**Replace** L foot leading partner to turn clockwise under left hand hold.	1	L hand hold extends out and up, R hand hold lowers
6	**Replace** R foot continuing to lead partner into wringer position.	2	L hand hold extends out and up
7	Step L foot **to the left** lowering left hand hold.	1	L hand hold encircles CW
8	Close R foot **to left foot** lowering left hand hold into wringer position.	2	L hand hold encircles CW
9-16	Step **forward** circling clockwise in wringer position.		
17	Step L foot **to the left** leading partner to turn counter-clockwise out of wringer position.	1	L hand hold encircles CW, R hand hold lowers
18	Step R foot **near left foot**.	2	L hand hold encircles CCW
19	**Replace** L foot completing wringer.	1	L hand hold encircles CCW and lowers
20	Close R foot **to left foot** returning to closed position.	2	L & R hand hold
21-24	Execute steps 1-4 of merengue basic.		

Step #5

Step #6

MERENGUE
Separation into Wringer
-Woman's Footwork-

Step	Description	Timing	Position
1	Step R foot **backward** beginning separation.	1	Closed into open
2	Step L foot **backward**.	2	Closed into open
3	Step R foot **backward** taking double hand hold.	1	Open, double hand hold
4	Close L foot **to right foot**.	2	Open, double hand hold
5	Step R foot **forward** (toe outward) beginning 3/4 turn clockwise into wringer.	1	Arch
6	Step L foot **around right foot**.	2	Arch
7	Step R foot **forward** (toe outward).	1	Arch into wringer
8	Step L foot **around right foot**.	2	Wringer
9-16	Step **forward** circling clockwise in wringer position.		
17	Step R foot **forward** (toe inward) beginning 3/4 turn counter-clockwise out of wringer.	1	Loop
18	Step L foot **forward** (toe outward).	2	Loop
19	Step R foot **around left foot** completing 3/4 turn left.	1	Loop, into open, double hand hold
20	Close L foot **to right foot**.	2	Double hand hold into closed
21-24	Execute steps 1-4 of merengue basic.		

Step #7

Step #8

MUSIC FOR MERENGUE

Los Hoyos de Bada

Merengue Merengue

Haitian Merengue

Pineapple Merengue

Hop, Skip Merengue

Sliding Merengue

Si Si Merengue

Tropical Merengue

BIBLIOGRAPHY

Ellfeldt, Lois, and Virgin L. Morton. <u>This is Ballroom Dance</u>. Palo Alto, California: National Press Book, 1974.

Fallow, Dennis Jr., and Sue Ann Kuchenmeister. <u>The Art of Ballroom Dance</u>. Minneapolis, Minnesota: Burgess Publishing Company, 1977.

Hill, Claudia. <u>American Social Dance</u>. Provo, Utah: Brigham Young University, 1985.

Kraus, Richard, Sarah Chapman Hilsendager and Brenda Dixon. <u>History of the Dance in Art and Education</u>. Englewood Cliffs, New Jersey: Prentice Hall, 1991.

Moute, John, and Bobbie Lawrence. <u>The Fred Astaire Dance Book</u>. New York, New York: Simon and Schuster, 1978.

Moore, Alex. <u>The Revised Technique of Ballroom Dancing</u>. London, England: Imperial Society of Teachers of Dancing, 1986.

Murray, Arthur. <u>How to Become a Good Dancer</u>. New York, New York: Simon and Schuster, 1959.

Stephenson, Richard M., and Joseph Iaccarino. <u>The Complete Book of Ballroom Dancing</u>. Garden City, New York: 1980.

Villacorte, Aurora I. <u>Step by Step to Ballroom Dancing</u>. Danville, Illinois: The Interstate Printers and Publishers, 1974.

Zelnik Geldys, Suzanne Marie. <u>The ABC's of Ballroom Dance</u>. Dubuque, Iowa: Kendall Hunt Publishing Company, 1991.